Reading Voyage 2

EXPERT

Reading *Voyage*
EXPERT 2

Publisher Chung Kyudo
Editor Jeong Yeonsoon
Authors Jonathan S. McClelland, Bin Walters
Proofreaders Michael A. Putlack, Mark Holden
Designer Design Sum

First published in April 2017
By Darakwon, Inc.
Darakwon Bldg., 211, Munbal-ro, Paju-si, Gyeonggi-do 10881
Republic of Korea
Tel: 82-2-736-2031 (Ext. 250)
Fax: 82-2-732-2037

Copyright © 2017 Darakwon, Inc.

All rights reserved. No part of this publication may be reproduced, stored in a retrieval system, or transmitted in any form or by any means, electronic, mechanical, photocopying or otherwise, without the prior consent of the copyright owner. Refund after purchase is possible only according to the company regulations. Contact the above telephone number for any inquiries. Consumer damages caused by loss, damage, etc. can be compensated according to the consumer dispute resolution standards announced by the Korea Fair Trade Commission. An incorrectly collated book will be exchanged.

ISBN 978-89-277-0781-3 58740
       978-89-277-0773-8 58740 (set)

www.darakwon.co.kr

Components Main Book / Workbook
10 9 8 7 6 5 4   23 24 25 26 27

Reading *Voyage*

EXPERT

2

Unit Components

Before You Read

This section helps students think about and predict the topic before reading the passage. It also enables students to better understand the reading passages by providing additional information related to the topic.

Main Reading Passage

A focus sentence gives students tips to help them understand the main idea of the text.

The passages are written to be as interesting and informative as possible, covering a variety of topics such as history, technology, and social issues.

Reading Skill

Students can review the key concepts of the passage by practicing various reading skills including identifying the main idea, sequencing, cause and effect, and more.

Vocabulary in Context

Students can learn the key words from the passage by matching them with their definitions and synonyms.

Reading Comprehension

This portion asks students to identify the main idea, details, and draw inferences from the passages through multiple-choice and short-answer questions.

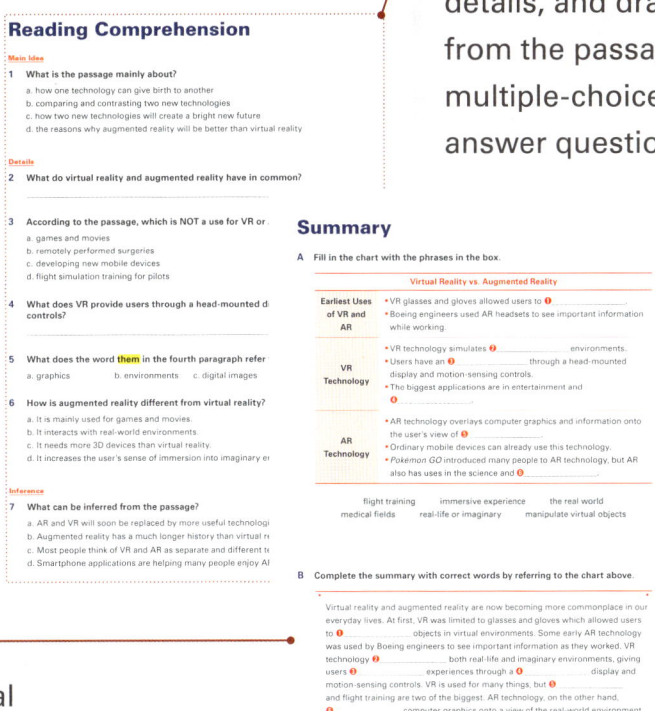

Summary

Students can review the essential information from the passage by filling in the graphic organizer and the summary.

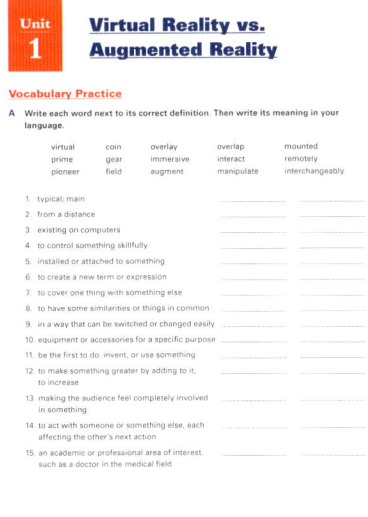

Workbook

Extra vocabulary and writing practice, and reading comprehension questions are provided to enable students to review the reading passages more deeply.

Online Supplement

MP3 files, answer keys, translations, and vocabulary lists are provided free online at www.darakwon.co.kr.

A program for generating vocabulary and writing test sheets is available free online at voca.darakwon.co.kr.

Table of Contents

Unit	Theme	Title	Reading Skill	Page
1	Technology	Virtual Reality vs. Augmented Reality	Compare & Contrast	9
2	History	Eye Makeup in Ancient Civilizations	Categorizing	15
3	Social Issues	The Continuing Problem of Slavery	Main Idea of Each Paragraph	21
4	Sociology	Urbanization and Its Results	Cause & Effect	27
5	Business	Why Businesses Offer Free Samples	Main Idea	33
6	History	The Chinese Terracotta Warriors	Sequencing	39
7	Social Issues	Terrorism, the New World War	Main Idea of Each Paragraph	45
8	Social Science	What IQ and EQ Tests Actually Determine	Compare & Contrast	51

Unit	Theme	Title	Reading Skill	Page
9	Literature	The Different Forms of Satire	Main Idea	57
10	Sociology	Natural Factors Influencing Development	Categorizing	63
11	Biology	The Eurasian Eagle-Owl	Main Idea of Each Paragraph	69
12	People	The Works of Louis Pasteur	Cause & Effect	75
13	Geology	The Difficulty of Predicting Earthquakes	Main Idea & Details	81
14	Linguistics	Writing Styles Around the World	Compare & Contrast	87
15	Technology	3D Printed Organs	Sequencing	93
16	Biology	Ocean Zones and Their Characteristics	Categorizing	99

Unit 1

Theme | *Technology*
Reading Skill | *Compare & Contrast*

Virtual Reality vs. Augmented Reality

Before You Read

A Think about the Topic

1. Do you think playing video games can give people useful skills?
2. What kind of information do you wish your phone could give you?

B Background Knowledge

Modern virtual reality is not the first time people have tried to create immersive environments. In the 19th century, 360-degree murals tried to put viewers "in the scene." At the same time, people were experimenting with two photos placed side by side and viewed with special glasses to make scenes look more realistic. These were limited to visual stimulation. In 1931, Edward Link used motion to engage the sense of touch when he patented the first flight simulator, the Link Trainer. It was a re-creation of an airplane cockpit that moved according to the "weather" and the "pilot's" actions. Nowadays, virtual reality combines physical sensations with computer graphics to put people in another world.

Unit 1
Technology | Compare & Contrast

Virtual Reality vs. Augmented Reality

▶ *While you read, consider how the technology and applications of virtual reality and augmented reality are similar and different.*

Two of the hottest topics in technology today are **virtual** reality (VR) and **augmented** reality (AR). These technologies are changing the way people **interact** with digital content. People often confuse the terms, using them interchangeably. Although VR and AR technologies **overlap** in some ways, there are several key differences between them.

The term "virtual reality" was coined in 1987 by computer scientist Jaron Lanier. His company pioneered research into 3D graphics and the first VR **gear**. It developed VR glasses and the data glove, a glove that users wore to manipulate objects in virtual worlds. A couple years later in 1990, Thomas Caudell, a researcher at the aircraft maker Boeing, came up with the term "augmented reality." He developed this term to describe a headset device that Boeing electricians wore. It would display graphical sets of directions while they laid out wires in very complex machines.

Both VR and AR rely on computer graphics and visual displays, but they utilize those technologies in opposite ways. As the name implies, virtual reality uses computer graphics to create a simulation of real life or imaginary environments. To accomplish this, VR is usually experienced through a head-mounted display and motion-sensing controls. This method of display provides a more **immersive** experience and makes users feel as if they are interacting with the environment firsthand. Today, VR is used for entertainment purposes, such as gaming and 3D movies. It is also used to provide training for real-life environments, such as flight *simulators for pilots.

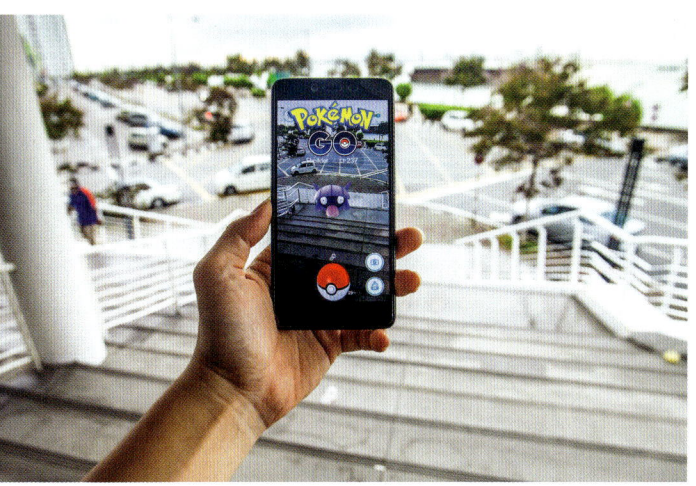

While VR technology creates a separate world, AR combines computer graphics and digital images with real environments. The graphics are used to enhance the environments by providing more information about **them**. Unlike VR, AR is more generally used via ordinary mobile devices such as smartphones and laptops. A prime example of the application of AR technology in our daily lives is the smartphone game *Pokémon GO*. The game takes various Pokémon characters and **overlays** them on a video image of the player's real-world environment. But AR is not just fun and games; it is also being used to enhance the fields of science and medicine. For instance, doctors might be able to use AR to perform surgeries **remotely**.

In the future, there is little doubt that both VR and AR technologies will become more commonplace. VR and AR are amazing technologies that provide a whole new level of interactions with digital worlds to make our lives easier. **Words 406**

*simulator: a training machine that gives users realistic experiences in a safe environment

Reading Skill

Comparing and contrasting is a way to explain how two or more things are similar and different.

Q What are the applications of virtual reality and augmented reality?
A Virtual reality is used in entertainment and _____ training while augmented reality is used in games and the science and _____ fields.

Vocabulary in Context

A Match the words in bold from the passage with their correct definitions.

1. _____ from a distance

2. _____ existing on computers

3. _____ to cover one thing with something else

4. _____ to have some similarities or things in common

5. _____ equipment or accessories for a specific purpose

6. _____ to make something greater by adding to it; to increase

7. _____ making the audience feel completely involved in something

8. _____ to act with someone or something else, each affecting the other's next action

B Look at the underlined words in the passage and choose the correct answers.

1. The word coin in the second paragraph is closest in meaning to _____.
   a. provide   b. decline   c. create   d. occur

2. The word manipulate in the second paragraph is closest in meaning to _____.
   a. affect   b. negotiate   c. enhance   d. control

3. The word imply in the third paragraph is closest in meaning to _____.
   a. suggest   b. realize   c. misuse   d. notice

4. The word firsthand in the third paragraph is closest in meaning to _____.
   a. directly   b. unusually   c. generally   d. exactly

C Choose the best word to complete each sentence.

1. The television was mounted / overlaid on the wall.

2. The application / applicant of new technologies often depends on the price.

3. We often see celebrities on TV but we rarely meet them firsthand / secondhand .

Reading Comprehension

Main Idea

1 What is the passage mainly about?

   a. how one technology can give birth to another
   b. comparing and contrasting two new technologies
   c. how two new technologies will create a bright new future
   d. the reasons why augmented reality will be better than virtual reality

Details

2 What do virtual reality and augmented reality have in common?

_____

3 According to the passage, which is NOT a use for VR or AR technology?

   a. games and movies
   b. remotely performed surgeries
   c. developing new mobile devices
   d. flight simulation training for pilots

4 What does VR provide users through a head-mounted display and motion-sensing controls?

_____

5 What does the word <mark>them</mark> in the fourth paragraph refer to?

   a. graphics   b. environments   c. digital images   d. mobile devices

6 How is augmented reality different from virtual reality?

   a. It is mainly used for games and movies.
   b. It interacts with real-world environments.
   c. It needs more 3D devices than virtual reality.
   d. It increases the user's sense of immersion into imaginary environments.

Inference

7 What can be inferred from the passage?

   a. AR and VR will soon be replaced by more useful technologies.
   b. Augmented reality has a much longer history than virtual reality.
   c. Most people think of VR and AR as separate and different technologies.
   d. Smartphone applications are helping many people enjoy AR technology.

Summary

A Fill in the chart with the phrases in the box.

	Virtual Reality vs. Augmented Reality
Earliest Uses of VR and AR	• VR glasses and gloves allowed users to ❶_____. • Boeing engineers used AR headsets to see important information while working.
VR Technology	• VR technology simulates ❷_____ environments. • Users have an ❸_____ through a head-mounted display and motion-sensing controls. • The biggest applications are in entertainment and ❹_____.
AR Technology	• AR technology overlays computer graphics and information onto the user's view of ❺_____. • Ordinary mobile devices can already use this technology. • *Pokémon GO* introduced many people to AR technology, but AR also has uses in the science and ❻_____.

flight training	immersive experience	the real world
medical fields	real-life or imaginary	manipulate virtual objects

B Complete the summary with correct words by referring to the chart above.

Virtual reality and augmented reality are now becoming more commonplace in our everyday lives. At first, VR was limited to glasses and gloves which allowed users to ❶_____ objects in virtual environments. Some early AR technology was used by Boeing engineers to see important information as they worked. VR technology ❷_____ both real-life and imaginary environments, giving users ❸_____ experiences through a ❹_____ display and motion-sensing controls. VR is used for many things, but ❺_____ and flight training are two of the biggest. AR technology, on the other hand, ❻_____ computer graphics onto a view of the real-world environment to display helpful information. Many people were ❼_____ to the power of AR by playing *Pokémon GO*, but it also has promising applications in the ❽_____ and medical fields.

Unit 2

Theme | *History*
Reading Skill | *Categorizing*

Eye Makeup in Ancient Civilizations

Before You Read

A Think about the Topic

1. Why do you think people wear makeup?
2. When do you think people first started wearing makeup?

B Background Knowledge

▲ The Eye of Horus

One of the earliest cultures to use makeup was ancient Egypt. This is reflected in their art, which depicts people wearing several types of makeup, as well as the Egyptian writing system, hieroglyphics. Perhaps the most prominent symbol depicting makeup is the Eye of Horus. The eye symbolizes protection, royal power, and good health. The symbol is a right eye with a curved tail coming from the bottom, a line extending to the left, and a teardrop. Egyptians often wore black makeup powder to recreate the Eye of Horus to protect themselves from the evil eye.

Unit 2
History | Categorizing

Eye Makeup in Ancient Civilizations

▶ *While you read, consider the changes in the reasons for wearing makeup over time.*

The evil eye, or the envious eye, is a widespread element of folklore traditions found throughout the world. It is thought to represent the sin of coveting, or jealousy. Anyone who is envious can unintentionally harm someone who is more fortunate simply by **gazing at** him or her with desire. Such a glance can **bestow** a **curse** that **afflicts** the receiver with poverty, disease, or even death.

Anthropologists believe the evil eye was a fundamental element in ancient Egyptian religion. The Egyptians took drastic measures to protect themselves. They would wear hand-shaped *amulets that possessed shielding powers. An extreme defense against the evil eye was mothers spitting in a stranger's face. This would protect their children by returning any curse sent by the envious person.

In ancient times, people also painted *kohl around their eyes to protect against the evil eye. The compound was created using special and sometime secret ingredients. It is tied to the origins of makeup, a substance used for facial beauty and skin protection. Its chemicals could also shield eyes from the harsh sunlight of the Egyptian desert. Kohl can even be seen in the **hieroglyphic** of the

Eye of Horus, a symbol of protection and power. It may have been the first documented use of eye makeup in history.

In ancient Greece, men and women from higher social classes would wear eye shadow for decorative purposes. They would apply ground charcoal mixed with olive oil and different colored herbs as eye shadow. Although the Greeks did not wear eye shadow for protection, they still believed that exaggerated eye shapes could ward off evil. For instance, archaeologists have uncovered sixth-century black-figured drinking **vessels** decorated with eyes. They believe the drawings were meant to prevent evil spirits from entering the drinker's body, protecting the drinker from consuming poison.

Eventually, cosmetics became common in and around the Mediterranean. They were used for entertainment and fashion. Stage actors used masks painted with kohl to symbolize characters since the masks made it easier for a large audience to see the actors' faces. As theater became more common, more people began wearing makeup. Over time, it was worn to enhance beauty by drawing attention to certain facial features. For instance, Roman women used mascara to make their eyelashes more **prominent**. The term mascara is derived from the Italian word *maschera*, meaning mask.

Words 391

*amulet: an object worn to protect against evil or harm
*kohl: a black powder that is put around the eyes

▲ A theatrical mask of ancient Rome

Reading Skill

Categorizing information means to arrange information or items into different groups.

Q   What are the different reasons ancient Egyptians and ancient Greeks used eye makeup?

A   The Egyptians wore dark cosmetics around their eyes as a way to _____ themselves from evil magic while the Greeks wore different colored cosmetics for _____ purposes.

Unit 2   17

Vocabulary in Context

A **Match the words or phrases in bold from the passage with their correct definitions.**

1. _____ an object used as a container

2. _____ a scientist who studies humans

3. _____ highly noticeable; well-known

4. _____ to give someone something

5. _____ to look at for a long time out of curiosity

6. _____ a writing system that uses pictures instead of words

7. _____ to affect someone badly and to make that person suffer

8. _____ magical words that are thought to cause harm or bad luck

B **Look at the underlined words or phrases in the passage and choose the correct answers.**

1. The word drastic in the second paragraph is closest in meaning to _____.
   a. effective   b. untested   c. extreme   d. typical

2. The word shield in the third paragraph is closest in meaning to _____.
   a. protect   b. disguise   c. reveal   d. confirm

3. The phrase ward off in the fourth paragraph is closest in meaning to _____.
   a. bring about   b. close down   c. put off   d. defend against

4. The word uncover in the fourth paragraph is closest in meaning to _____.
   a. produce   b. discover   c. inform   d. announce

C **Choose the best word to complete each sentence.**

1. My cat likes to glance / gaze out the window and watch the people walk by.

2. The president bestowed / obtained a trophy and a $10,000 check on the winner.

3. After years of making movies and winning awards, Dave became a prominent / promising and famous director.

Reading Comprehension

Main Idea

1. **What is the passage mainly about?**

   a. the history of cosmetics in ancient Egypt

   b. superstitions in ancient cultures that still exist today

   c. the origin and purpose of eye makeup in various societies

   d. methods ancient people used to protect themselves from curses

Details

2. **What was the evil eye according to the passage?**

   a. It was an amulet given to others.

   b. It was a look that cursed the receiver.

   c. It was a defense against the attacks of others.

   d. It was the most prominent religious symbol in Greece.

3. **What was the initial purpose of kohl?**

   _____

4. **Which of the following is true according to the passage?**

   a. The Egyptians wore amulets shaped like the Eye of Horus for protection.

   b. Mascara was used by women in Rome to enhance their facial features.

   c. Eye makeup was usually worn by impoverished women in ancient Greece.

   d. People in Egypt covered their bodies with kohl to protect themselves from the sun.

5. **What does the word it in the fifth paragraph refer to?**

   a. kohl   b. audience   c. theater   d. makeup

6. **Why did actors in the Mediterranean wear masks?**

   _____

Inference

7. **What can be inferred from the passage?**

   a. Poison was often used in ancient Greece to murder people.

   b. People in Rome wore cosmetics as a form of protection against evil.

   c. The ancient Egyptians believed that the evil eye cursed envious people.

   d. People in the Mediterranean wore eye shadow to look like performers.

Unit 2 19

Summary

A Fill in the chart with the phrases in the box.

	Eye Makeup in Ancient Civilizations
Ancient Egypt	• People in ancient Egypt painted kohl around their eyes to shield themselves ❶_____ and the harsh sunlight of the desert. • The kohl compound is seen in the hieroglyphic of the Eye of Horus.
Ancient Greece	• ❷_____ men and women in ancient Greece wore makeup made from charcoal around their eyes for ❸_____. • Some drinking containers were decorated with eyes so that the users would be ❹_____ evil spirits and poison.
In and Around the Mediterranean	• Stage actors began to ❺_____ painted with kohl to make it easier for audiences to see their faces. • Women in ancient Rome wore mascara to make their eyelashes ❻_____.

upper-class   wear masks   against the evil eye
more prominent   protected from   decorative purposes

B Complete the summary with correct words by referring to the chart above.

Cosmetic eye makeup developed from an ancient belief in the ❶_____. It was thought that harm could be inflicted on someone by looking at that person ❷_____. To ❸_____ themselves against the evil eye, the ancient Egyptians painted a compound made of ❹_____ around their eyes. This compound is seen in the hieroglyphic of the Eye of Horus, which symbolized protection and ❺_____. The ancient Greeks wore cosmetics around their eyes for decorative purposes. However, they still believed that drinking vessels ❻_____ with eyes could protect them from evil spirits and ❼_____. Over time, cosmetics became fashionable as actors started using masks painted with kohl and women wore cosmetics to enhance certain facial ❽_____.

Unit 3

Theme | *Social Issues*
Reading Skill | *Main Idea of Each Paragraph*

The Continuing Problem of Slavery

Before You Read

A Think about the Topic

1. Do you think it is ever okay to do work for free?
2. What country or countries do you think have the most slaves today?

B Background Knowledge

Usually, when people talk about slavery, they are talking about the past. For example, the ancient Romans were famous for many things, including their extensive use of slaves from captured lands. In addition, slavery was a massive and regulated part of the United States economy little more than a hundred and fifty years ago and it was also common in many other countries. Nowadays, most people do not know anybody who is a slave, so they may think the problem has gone away even though it could be in their backyards.

Unit 3
Social Issues | Main Idea of Each Paragraph

The Continuing Problem of Slavery

▶ *As you read, consider the places where slavery is a major problem and why it continues to exist.*

Slavery has existed since before written history. The first people to have been **enslaved** were likely some individuals living during *Neolithic Revolution. In the millennia since, virtually every country and culture has hosted some form of slavery. Today, slavery is <u>outlawed</u> in practically every nation, yet this horrible practice continues as millions of people of all ages remain enslaved around the world.

The number of slaves globally is estimated to be between 21 and 46 million people. While slavery exists in all regions of the world, it is the most predominant in Asia and Africa. A study by the Walk Free Foundation, an anti-slavery organization, reported that India had the highest number of slaves, totaling 18 million. China has the next highest number of slaves at nearly three and a half million, followed by Pakistan, Bangladesh, and Uzbekistan. Other countries with a high proportion of slaves are North Korea, Iran, and Sudan. Slavery <u>persists</u> in these countries due to the **lax** enforcement of anti-slavery laws or, in the case of North Korea, government **sanctioning** of the practice.

Just as slavery exists in many places, there are many reasons that people are enslaved. Perhaps the most widespread type of slavery is forced labor. This is when people are forced to do work, often with no payment, against their will under the threat of some form of punishment. It most frequently occurs in labor-intensive and under-regulated industries, including agriculture and fishing; domestic work; construction, mining, **quarrying**, and brick *kilns; and manufacturing. Perhaps the oldest form of slavery is **bonded** labor. This is when people are asked to work to repay a debt. Even though the value of their labor often exceeds the amount of their debt, bonded laborers work for little or no pay. In many cases, the debts are passed onto the following generations, meaning that the children of bonded laborers must become bonded laborers themselves.

There is hope for the millions of people enslaved around the world. National governments are **clamping down on** slaveholders. For instance, in 2007 the Chinese government freed 550 people enslaved by brick manufacturers, with 69 children included among them. The government has assembled a force of 35,000 police officers to check brick kilns throughout the country to prevent human **trafficking**. Non-government organizations (NGOs) such as Anti-Slavery International work on the **grassroots** level to influence political leaders and to enact changes worldwide. You can donate your time and money to these organizations to banish slavery from our world once and for all. **Words 416**

*Neolithic Revolution: the transition from a lifestyle based on hunting to a lifestyle of agriculture and settlement
*kiln: a type of large oven used for making clay objects

Reading Skill

The main idea of each paragraph gives a general idea that is explained in the rest of the paragraph.

Q What is the main idea of paragraph 4?
A There have been efforts by governments and NGOs to _____ modern slavery.

Vocabulary in Context

A Match the words or phrases in bold from the passage with their correct definitions.

1. _____ to make someone a slave
2. _____ to officially permit or approve
3. _____ not strict or careful about rules
4. _____ obligated by a debt to serve without wages
5. _____ the act of buying and selling something illegally
6. _____ the business or activity of digging stones out of the ground
7. _____ to take action to stop an activity or the people doing an activity
8. _____ the lowest level of organization, usually involving common people

B Look at the underlined words in the passage and choose the correct answers.

1. The word outlaw in the first paragraph is closest in meaning to _____.
   a. allow   b. legalize   c. accept   d. prohibit

2. The word persist in the second paragraph is closest in meaning to _____.
   a. insist   b. encounter   c. continue   d. stop

3. The word assemble in the fourth paragraph is closest in meaning to _____.
   a. associate   b. gather   c. order   d. set up

4. The word banish in the fourth paragraph is closest in meaning to _____.
   a. recognize   b. expel   c. disappear   d. prevent

C Choose the best word to complete each sentence.

1. Despite being outlawed, slavery sustains / persists around the world.
2. Our school has assembled / disassembled a great basketball team this year.
3. The suspect vanished / banished while police were chasing him, and he has yet to be found.

24

Reading Comprehension

Main Idea

1. **What is the passage mainly about?**

   a. the reasons why slavery should be against the law

   b. the reasons for and locations of modern slavery

   c. the reasons why people purchase slaves in modern times

   d. the best ways to avoid becoming enslaved in the modern world

Details

2. **According to the passage, which country has the most slaves?**

   _____

3. **What does the word It in the third paragraph refer to?**

   a. threat   b. their will   c. forced labor   d. punishment

4. **What is the main reason slavery persists according to the passage?**

   a. many countries sanctioning slavery

   b. too many people with too much debt

   c. lax enforcement of laws against slavery

   d. not enough people willing to work in dirty jobs

5. **Which of the following is NOT true according to the passage?**

   a. Iran and Sudan have taken little action to end slavery.

   b. Some children are enslaved to repay their parents' debts.

   c. The top five countries with the most slaves are all Asian countries.

   d. The oldest form of slavery is forced labor in labor-intensive industries.

6. **Why do NGOs work on the grassroots level?**

   _____

Inference

7. **What CANNOT be inferred from the passage?**

   a. Many countries officially sanction bonded labor.

   b. There is a lot of work left to end the practice of slavery.

   c. Some people become forced laborers through human trafficking.

   d. Some Asian and African countries have to strengthen their anti-slavery laws.

Unit 3 25

Summary

A Fill in the chart with the phrases in the box.

The Continuing Problem of Slavery	
Where ❶ _____	• India leads the world, with 18 million slaves. • China, Pakistan, Bangladesh, and Uzbekistan also have a high number of slaves.
Reasons for Slavery	• Forced labor persists in places with lax enforcement of ❷ _____ for activities like agriculture, mining, and manufacturing. • Many people fall into debt and become trapped in bonded labor to ❸ _____. • This bonded labor can continue ❹ _____.
Efforts to Clamp Down	• The Chinese government has assembled a force of 35,000 police officers to prevent ❺ _____ and to inspect industries. • NGOs work at the ❻ _____ to influence political leaders and to effect changes around the world. • You can volunteer time and money to help out.

pay it back	human trafficking	grassroots level
slavery persists	across generations	industrial regulations

B Complete the summary with correct words by referring to the chart above.

Despite being almost universally ❶ _____, slavery continues to persist. India, with 18 million slaves, leads the world. Other Asian countries, like China, Pakistan, Bangladesh, and Uzbekistan, also have a high number of slaves. ❷ _____ labor, the most widespread type of slavery, continues because of lax ❸ _____ of industrial regulations. Other people fall into ❹ _____, and their labor is the only way to pay it back. This is called ❺ _____ labor, and it can continue across generations. However, national governments are ❻ _____ down. For example, the Chinese government has ❼ _____ a police force to prevent human trafficking and to monitor industries. At the grassroots level, NGOs work to ❽ _____ political leaders. Ending slavery is a cooperative effort, and you can do your part by volunteering your time and money.

Unit 4

Theme | *Sociology*
Reading Skill | *Cause & Effect*

Urbanization and Its Results

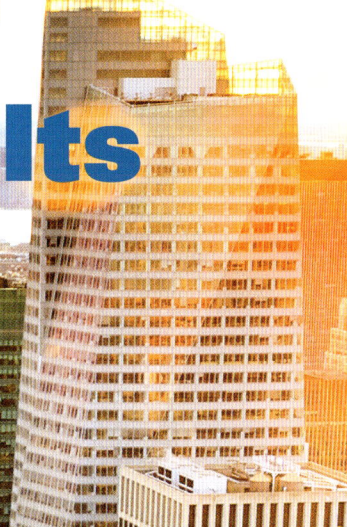

Before You Read

A Think about the Topic

1. Why do people want to move to big cities?
2. What problems are associated with large urban areas?

B Background Knowledge

For most of human history, people lived in rural areas and depended on agriculture to survive. For instance, in 1800, just three percent of the world's population lived in urban areas. Starting with the Industrial Revolution, cities like London and New York began to grow rapidly. By 1900, around 14 percent of people lived in urban regions, and 12 cities around the world had populations of more than one million. Urban growth continued, and by 1950, 30 percent of the world's population was urbanites, with 83 cities having populations over one million. The year 2008 marked a turning point, with half of citizens globally living in cities. This urbanization trend is likely to continue.

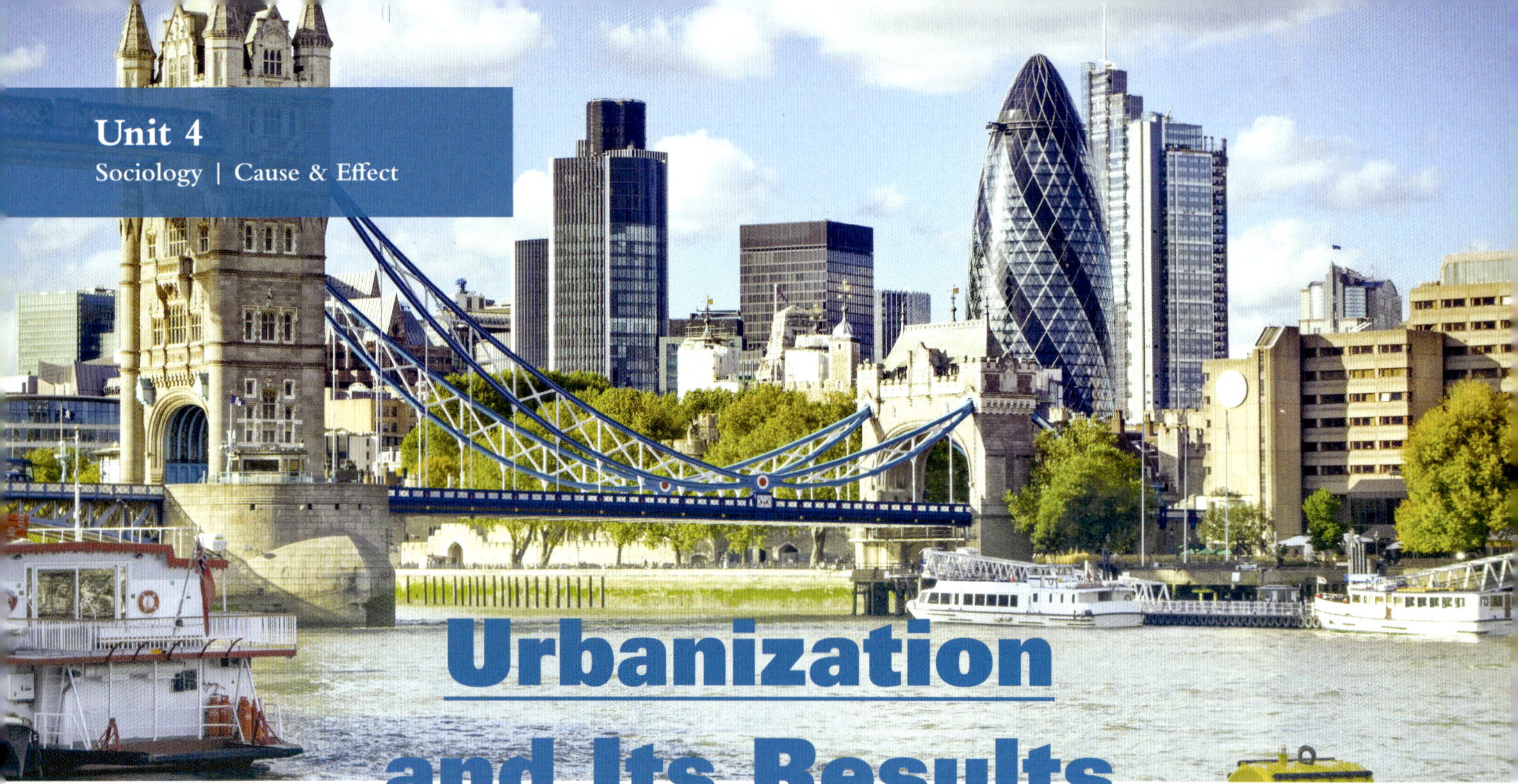

Unit 4
Sociology | Cause & Effect

Urbanization and Its Results

▶ *While you read, pay attention to what changes occurred due to the increase of London's population.*

Urbanization is the large-scale **influx** of people into cities. Large population movements create tremendous demand for goods and services. New businesses arise to take advantage of the new workers and consumers. Government services of all kinds develop to keep order and to meet the needs of the ever-growing population. The increasing consumer demand accompanying urbanization causes prices to rise, particularly in **real estate**. Many poor and working class residents are **priced out of the housing market** and are forced to move into low-rent areas.

The classic example of modern urbanization is London in the late nineteenth century. In the late 1800s, London was becoming a much more interesting place. Tens of thousands of people were moving in every year, leading to a huge **demographic** transformation. There was massive construction of housing to **accommodate** the newcomers, with everything from inexpensive **tenements** to luxury single family homes being built. Construction for the commercial sector, mainly offices and factories, increased tremendously. Untold thousands of new businesses started, bringing about an economic boom and creating enormous new wealth.

28

Governing London became a very complex undertaking. The city government had to make sure the newly built residential and commercial areas were connected by roads. Soon, the existing roads were not enough, and no realistic road construction plan could meet the demand for transportation. Thus, London began building the world's first underground railway system in 1854. By 1880, it was carrying 40 million passengers a year. The City of London, the financial district within London, became home to an **array** of financial enterprises. ==The most famous== is the London Stock Exchange. Decisions made in the City have always had a great effect on the global economy, and London became the world's foremost industrial and commercial center.

▲ The Royal Stock Exchange in London

The new urban growth created a city sharply divided by social class. The number of wealthy people grew from the fabulous profits of the new businesses and land rents. The middle class also expanded because the economy needed technical specialists, managers, lawyers, and other professionals. Businesses required a great deal of new office and storage space. These factors caused rents to rise dramatically, and many houses in central London were worth millions of dollars in today's prices. These developments made it impossible for the city's poor and working class majority to live in the central areas, so most residents had to move out of the city center into areas informally designated for the less **well-off**. Words 405

Reading Skill

Cause and effect is when one event causes something to happen. The cause explains why something happens, and the effect is what happens as a result.

Q   Why did the London government decide to build an underground railway system?
A   They built it since the existing _____ were not adequate and there was no realistic road construction plan to meet the _____.

Vocabulary in Context

A **Match the words or phrases in bold from the passage with their correct definitions.**

1. _____ land or buildings
2. _____ a large group or variety of things
3. _____ related to population patterns
4. _____ having plenty of money; wealthy
5. _____ to provide room for someone to stay
6. _____ the arrival of a large number of people or things
7. _____ a large building divided into apartments for the urban poor
8. _____ to make a price too high for certain groups of people to afford

B **Look at the underlined words in the passage and choose the correct answers.**

1. The word untold in the second paragraph is closest in meaning to _____.
   a. inadequate   b. imaginable   c. uncountable   d. limited

2. The word undertaking in the third paragraph is closest in meaning to _____.
   a. task   b. attempt   c. assessment   d. priority

3. The word fabulous in the fourth paragraph is closest in meaning to _____.
   a. honorable   b. believable   c. typical   d. superb

4. The word designate in the fourth paragraph is closest in meaning to _____.
   a. name   b. locate   c. seek   d. place

C **Choose the best word to complete each sentence.**

1. Today, computer graphics almost look completely practical / realistic .

2. Children under the age of 10 must be accompanied / accomplished by an adult on this ride.

3. The U.S. economy experienced a(n) boom / escalation in the late 1990s followed by a downturn.

Reading Comprehension

Main Idea

1 **What is the passage mainly about?**

   a. the growth of London's underground transportation and financial district

   b. the concept of urbanization as demonstrated by nineteenth-century London

   c. how the London city government dealt with urbanization in the nineteenth century

   d. increasing class divisions resulting from urbanization in nineteenth-century London

Details

2 **Which of the following is NOT true about urbanization according to the passage?**

   a. It leads to the separation of social classes.

   b. It brings about the growth of business.

   c. It has little effect on consumer prices.

   d. It creates an increasing need for transportation.

3 **What did London do in response to the city's demographic transformation?**

   _____

4 **What does the phrase The most famous in the third paragraph refer to?**

   a. financial district   b. London

   c. railway system   d. financial enterprises

5 **How did London deal with the new demand for transportation?**

   _____

6 **According to paragraph 4, urban growth _____.**

   a. encouraged people to invest more money in stock

   b. allowed business owners to reduce spending on rent

   c. reduced the demand for skilled workers such as lawyers

   d. forced impoverished citizens into areas outside the city center

Inference

7 **What can be inferred from the passage?**

   a. Urbanization caused large inequalities in wealth and income.

   b. Most businesses in London dealt with the financial sector.

   c. Middle class people could not afford to buy property in London.

   d. Office buildings were built outside the city center due to high rents.

Summary

A Fill in the chart with the phrases in the box.

Urbanization and Its Results	
The Case of London	• In the late 1800s, tens of thousands of people moved into London, causing a huge ❶_____. • The city underwent a ❷_____ of housing and commercial buildings to accommodate the demand.
Governing the City	• The road system could not meet the ❸_____, so the city constructed the world's first underground railway system. • The financial center of the city, the City of London, became the world's leading financial and ❹_____.
The Effects on Social Classes	• As a result of the ❺_____ from businesses and rents, the number of wealthy people grew as did the number of skilled middle-class professionals. • Due to the ❻_____, most poor and working class people were forced to move far outside the city center.

| huge profits | demand for transportation | massive construction |
| rising rents | demographic transformation | commercial center |

B Complete the summary with correct words by referring to the chart above.

❶_____ occurs when a great number of people move into cities, creating an increased demand for ❷_____ and services. Rising consumer demand leads to ❸_____ prices, which creates changes to social demographics. In the nineteenth century, London experienced an ❹_____ of people moving into the city. This required the massive construction of ❺_____ and commercial buildings. To meet increased transportation demands, the city built the world's first underground ❻_____ system. By this time, the City of London had become the world's leading financial center. As a result of the success of businesses, the number of wealthy and ❼_____ class people grew. However, rising rents forced ❽_____ class people to move away from the city center.

Unit 5

Theme | *Business*
Reading Skill | *Main Idea*

Why Businesses Offer Free Samples

Before You Read

A Think about the Topic

1. What do you think the purpose of offering free samples is?
2. How do you think businesses can make money by giving away their products?

B Background Knowledge

The sole goal of nearly every business is to make as much money as possible. Knowing this, the idea of giving away free samples of a product would make little sense. But companies think about the long-term effects of giving away free samples. By letting consumers try out their products at no cost, companies are exposing their products to countless customers who may never have tried the items otherwise. By doing this, companies hope to create lifelong customers. This is just one of the reasons that giving away products for free is such an effective business strategy.

Unit 5
Business | Main Idea

Why Businesses Offer Free Samples

▶ *As you read, consider the different benefits businesses get by offering free samples.*

Customers love getting **freebies**, and for this reason companies will frequently hand out **complimentary** drinks, desserts, and more. While offering their product for free may seem like poor business strategy, it is one of the most effective ways to create brand **awareness** and to boost product sales.

Free samples are effective since they <u>compel</u> people to buy more. Whenever people receive something free, they feel **obliged** to **reciprocate** the **generosity** of this act. This is why, contrary to logic, companies that give away freebies will actually have higher sales. For example, one American convenience store chain gives away free small iced drinks one day each year. <u>Presumably</u>, people would come in, get their free drink, and leave, but this is often not the case. After having the free drink, people often buy a larger version of the drink during their visit. The company reports that its sales increase by 40 percent on the day of the giveaway.

Researchers have also found that people are willing to pay a high price for a product later if they get it free <u>initially</u>. When something is inexpensive, people often perceive the item as being of low quality, and they always hold on to this perception. However, when something is given away free—does not have a price attached to it—we look for other signs that indicate value. If your main purchase is a high-quality, expensive item, then you will **associate** any item you receive with it as being the same quality. For instance, customers who purchase luxury brand cosmetics often receive free samples along with their purchases. Even though they do not cost anything, the customers will consider them to be of the same quality as their main purchases and be willing to pay **top dollar** for them later.

The final benefit of freebies is the increase in word-of-mouth marketing. Due to the rise of social media, companies have realized the power of having customers spread the word about their products online. People sometimes use social networking sites to share their experiences using certain products with their friends, thereby increasing awareness of those brands. Companies have found that the most effective way of getting customers to talk about their products with their friends is to give them away. For instance, one article in the *Journal of Marketing* found that those who got a product for free were 20 percent more likely to talk about it, and those who got a freebie tied to the product talked about it 15 percent more often. **Words 420**

Reading Skill

*The **main idea** is usually at the beginning of a text and makes a general statement.*

Q   What is the main idea of the passage?
A   Businesses sometimes give _____ products to make customers aware of their brands and to _____ sales.

Vocabulary in Context

A   Match the words or phrases in bold from the passage with their correct definitions.

1. _____ given for free

2. _____ a very high price

3. _____ something given away at no cost

4. _____ the state of knowing about something

5. _____ feeling that you must do something

6. _____ the act of treating someone well; kindness

7. _____ to think of one thing along with something else

8. _____ to do something for someone who has done something for you

B   Look at the underlined words in the passage and choose the correct answers.

1. The word compel in the second paragraph is closest in meaning to _____.
   a. serve   b. motivate   c. compromise   d. threaten

2. The word presumably in the second paragraph is closest in meaning to _____.
   a. especially   b. apparently   c. certainly   d. immediately

3. The word initially in the third paragraph is closest in meaning to _____.
   a. probably   b. significantly   c. at once   d. at first

4. The word perception in the third paragraph is closest in meaning to _____.
   a. belief   b. kindness   c. observation   d. concept

C   Choose the best word or phrase to complete each sentence.

1. All passengers on the plane receive complimentary / complementary food and drinks.

2. It is important to increase awareness / association of your cause if you want people to join it.

3. Although she didn't agree with us at first, she eventually gave away / gave in to our requests.

Reading Comprehension

Main Idea

1. What is the passage mainly about?

   a. how the price of an item affects people's perception of it
   b. a sales strategy that goes against logic but actually works
   c. different methods that companies use to create brand awareness
   d. the advantages and disadvantages of giving away free products

Details

2. In paragraph 2, the author states that _____.

   a. American convenience stores often give away free iced drinks
   b. people want to pay back companies that give them something free
   c. most customers only get the free iced drink without making a purchase
   d. 40 percent of customers prefer getting free drinks with their purchases

3. What does the word they in the third paragraph refer to?

   a. customers
   b. main purchases
   c. free samples
   d. luxury brand cosmetics

4. Why are people willing to pay a lot of money later for free cosmetic samples?

   _____

5. How does social networking increase awareness of a brand?

   _____

6. Which of the following is NOT true according to the passage?

   a. People believe that items that are not expensive are low quality.
   b. One convenience store sells more iced drinks by giving them away.
   c. Companies want their customers to talk about their products online.
   d. People are more likely to talk about freebies connected to a product they purchase.

Inference

7. What can be inferred from the passage?

   a. Most people buy only products when they get freebies with them.
   b. The majority of freebies are given away by cosmetics companies.
   c. Most free product promotions occur on social networking websites.
   d. Companies can make more money from free products than inexpensive ones.

Summary

A Fill in the chart with the phrases in the box.

	Why Businesses Offer Free Samples
Compel People to Buy More	• People ❶_____ to purchase a product whenever they receive something free. • One American convenience store chain sells 40 percent more iced drinks on the day it gives the drink away each year.
People Are Willing to Pay More Later	• People perceive inexpensive items to be of ❷_____, but they look for other signs to ❸_____ of an item that is free. • Customers who purchase luxury brand cosmetics will associate the free samples they receive with the ❹_____ they purchase and are willing to pay a lot for them later.
Increase in ❺_____ Marketing	• Customers today use ❻_____ to share their experiences using a product with their friends. • One study found that people who got a free product were 20 percent more likely to talk about it.

low quality   word-of-mouth   feel obligated
social media   high-quality items   indicate the value

B Complete the summary with correct words by referring to the chart above.

Businesses often provide ❶_____ samples of their products to help ❷_____ their sales. One reason is that it ❸_____ people to buy more. Customers feel ❹_____ to purchase products after getting something free. For instance, one American convenience store chain sells 40 percent more iced drinks on the day it gives them ❺_____. Free items also make people willing to ❻_____ more for them later. People consider inexpensive items to be of ❼_____ quality, but when customers get a free item along with an expensive product, they consider it to be high quality. Finally, free samples lead to more word-of-mouth advertising. People who receive a free item are more likely to talk about it with their ❽_____ online.

Unit 6

Theme | *History*
Reading Skill | *Sequencing*

The Chinese Terracotta Warriors

Before You Read

A Think about the Topic

1. What do you know about the Terracotta Warriors?
2. What do you think the purpose of the figures was?

B Background Knowledge

China's first emperor, Ying Zheng, better known by his self-given name of Qin Shi Huang, helped to create China as we think of it today. He was the first emperor of a unified China, ruling from 221 B.C. to 210 B.C. Qin is credited with pulling together the whole of China at a time when it was just a collection of warring states. In fact, Qin began many reforms, including the organization of a sophisticated government. He also unified Chinese writing and currency. He is famously remembered, however, for his efforts to enhance a defensive line that would later become the Great Wall of China and his massive army of terracotta warriors.

Unit 6
History | Sequencing

The Chinese Terracotta Warriors

▶ *As you read, pay attention to the methods used to create the Terracotta warrior army.*

Chinese farmers in Shaanxi Province made an amazing discovery when digging up a field to make a well in 1974. Underneath the ground, they found an ancient army of life-sized and lifelike clay figures. This army is now known as the Terracotta Warriors. Built for the first emperor of China Qin Shi Huang in 246 B.C., they stood guard in his **mausoleum** to protect and serve him in the afterlife. Historians estimate that it took 700,000 workers 38 years to build the entire **edifice**. Yet it is the soldiers that continue to inspire and awe visitors who come to see them.

The construction of the warriors mostly took place in northern China near the site of the tomb. The area had an abundance of clay and *loess, which is extremely flexible and **adhesive** and is ideal for the creation of statues. Work on the figures proceeded in a series of stages. The feet were **fashioned** first on a square base with the legs added afterward. Once partially dry, strips of clay were wound upward to create a hollow body with the exterior smoothed out using flat paddles. Then, various tools were used to create the appearance of armor on the flattened surface.

Next, the heads and hands were pasted on the **torso**. While each head was generic, it underwent a complicated procedure to make it unique. Each of the 8,000 warriors has a different face. Individual features were created with molds that were later **stylized** by hand. The figures are also different heights depending on their roles, with generals being the tallest figures. Each soldier was also given actual weapons made of bronze, which were quite advanced for the period and contributed to their realism.

Also at the site were the large kilns needed to fire the terracotta figures. Researchers believe that the kilns reached temperatures between 800 to 900 degrees Celsius. The heat had to be carefully controlled since higher temperatures would have caused the clay to become uneven while lower temperatures would have made the figures brittle. Afterward, gelatin or raw *lacquer was applied to give flesh tones, and the eyes were painted with black **pupils** and brown **irises** to give the statues lifelike appearances. Despite understanding the processes, researchers are still unable to replicate these stunning figures.

Words 380

*loess: a fine soil that is usually yellow or brown and is deposited by the wind
*lacquer: a liquid which is painted on a substance and forms a shiny surface when it dries

Reading Skill

Sequencing is putting events in order from first to last. When we sequence, we can easily understand which events happen first, second, and so on.

Q   In what order was each warrior constructed?

A   The first step was creating _____ on a base and adding the legs, after which strips of clay were added to create a _____. Finally, the head and hands were added.

Vocabulary in Context

A **Match the words in bold from the passage with their correct definitions.**

1. _____ a large building or structure

2. _____ the colored, round part of the eye

3. _____ to make something using one's hands

4. _____ the black, round area in the center of the eye

5. _____ being sticky and able to hold other things together

6. _____ a building in which the bodies of dead people are buried

7. _____ the main part of the human body without the head, arms, or legs

8. _____ to make something look like a pattern or type rather than appear natural

B **Look at the underlined words in the passage and choose the correct answers.**

1. The word awe in the first paragraph is closest in meaning to _____.
   a. annoy   b. concern   c. shock   d. amaze

2. The word hollow in the second paragraph is closest in meaning to _____.
   a. hard   b. empty   c. frequent   d. useless

3. The word generic in the third paragraph is closest in meaning to _____.
   a. obvious   b. common   c. diversified d. comprehensive

4. The word brittle in the fourth paragraph is closest in meaning to _____.
   a. fragile   b. tough   c. rusty   d. permanent

C **Choose the best word to complete each sentence.**

1. It is easy to get lost in this town since it has so many generic / genetic buildings.

2. Many people undertake / undergo substantial changes after they go away to college.

3. Because she did not process / possess the necessary documents, she could not enter the country.

Reading Comprehension

Main Idea

1 **What is the passage mainly about?**

   a. the discovery of an ancient art gallery in China
   b. religious practices that originated in ancient China
   c. the process of making clay figures in ancient China
   d. the various forms of Chinese pottery throughout history

Details

2 **What does the word them in the first paragraph refer to?**

   a. visitors   b. soldiers   c. historians   d. workers

3 **According to the passage, what purpose did the Terracotta Warriors serve?**

   a. They kept intruders out of the tomb.
   b. They protected the king in the afterlife.
   c. They scared away ghosts in the mausoleum.
   d. They supported the edifice of the king's tomb.

4 **Why did the construction of the warriors take place near the tomb?**

_____

5 **Which of the following is NOT true about the appearance of the warriors?**

   a. Each warrior was given a piece of armor made of bronze.
   b. The heights of each of the warrior figures were not the same.
   c. The figures were covered in gelatin to give them a skin-like color.
   d. The appearance of armor was created before pasting the heads on the body.

6 **What would happen if the temperature in the kilns was too high?**

_____

Inference

7 **What can be inferred about the construction of the warriors from the passage?**

   a. The features were completely created by hand.
   b. The faces were made to look similar to each other.
   c. The Chinese had knowledge of advanced weaponry.
   d. The weapons were created in the same way as the figures.

Unit 6   43

Summary

A Fill in the chart with the phrases in the box.

The Terracotta Warriors	
The Construction Process	• The warriors were built in northern China near the site of the tomb since the area had ❶_____ and loess. • Each figure was built using a step-by-step process starting with ❷_____ and ending with the heads.
Making the Figures Unique	• Each soldier had a ❸_____ that was later stylized by hand to give it a unique appearance. • The soldiers were also given real ❹_____ to make them seem more authentic.
The Use of Kilns	• Kilns heated to between 800 and 900 degrees Celsius were used to ❺_____. • If the temperature was too high, the clay would be uneven while lower temperatures would ❻_____.

the feet   abundant clay   bake the clay
generic face   make it brittle   bronze weapons

B Complete the summary with correct words by referring to the chart above.

The Terracotta Warriors were built for China's first emperor Qin Shi Huang to guard his tomb. The warriors were constructed near the ❶_____ in northern China. Made of ❷_____ and loess, the figures were constructed step-by-step starting with the feet and ending with the heads. Each soldier was ❸_____ by hand to give it a unique appearance. Soldiers were also given real bronze ❹_____, adding to their authenticity. ❺_____ were used to fire the terracotta warriors. The kilns had to be kept at a specific ❻_____ to make sure the clay did not become ❼_____ or too brittle. While researchers understand the process by which the soldiers were made, they have not been able to ❽_____ the figures.

Unit 7

Theme | *Social Issues*
Reading Skill | *Main Idea of Each Paragraph*

Terrorism, the New World War

Before You Read

A Think about the Topic

1. What are some terrorist attacks that you know about?
2. Why do you think people become terrorists?

B Background Knowledge

The word "terrorism" was coined to describe the horrible actions that revolutionaries used against their opponents during the French Revolution. In 1858, an Italian fighter named Felice Orsini threw three bombs to kill Napoleon III. The attack, in which eight people died and 142 were injured, served as an inspiration for later terrorist attacks. The Irish Republican Brotherhood was one of the first groups to carry out a modern terrorist attack. The group placed explosives throughout Britain to achieve its political goals. By the early 20th century, terrorism became clearly defined. Today, it is one of the most serious threats to the peace of our world.

Unit 7
Social Issues | Main Idea of Each Paragraph

Terrorism, the New World War

▶ As you read, think about how the methods and effects of terrorism differ from traditional wars.

    Global conflicts such as World War I and II have been absent from our world for over 70 years. However, another and perhaps more frightening form of warfare has emerged in its place: terrorism. Terrorism can occur almost anytime, anywhere, and it is for this reason that it is so alarming to many people.

5   Broadly defined, terrorism is the use of **indiscriminate** violence by non-government groups to **instill** fear into the public to fulfill political, religious, or ideological goals. Terrorists often attack visible targets that symbolize what they oppose. This draws the attention of the public and governments to their acts. For instance, at the 1972 Munich Olympics, 11 Israelis were killed by the Black September Organization, a Palestinian terrorist
10 organization. While the Israelis were the immediate victims, the one billion people watching the event were the true targets.

▲ The Pentagon shortly after terrorist attacks

    From 2000 to 2014, over 61,000 terrorist attacks were carried out, claiming the lives of 140,000 victims. Among the most significant acts of terrorism were the attacks on
15 September 11, 2001. This is when the terrorist group Al-Qaeda hijacked four commercial airliners and crashed them into the New York World Trade Center and Pentagon. However, most

go unnoticed by the majority of people globally. During this same period, nearly 16,000 terrorist attacks occurred in Iraq alone. Another 9,700 and 7,600 such incidents occurred in Pakistan and Afghanistan respectively.

Terrorist groups actively try to recruit new members. Many terrorists come from the lower social classes or **alienated** groups in society. They are drawn to become terrorists by a sense of **altruism**, which makes them believe that they are part of an organization doing good for the world. Having a sense of **self-righteous** sacrifice allows them to justify the violence they commit. Terrorists may also believe themselves to be victims of society. They feel that becoming terrorists is the only way to fix the problems they see in the world.

The United States and other nations have initiated a "war on terror" in response to these threats. Also referred to as counter-terrorism measures, anti-terrorism laws have given hundreds of government organizations the means to collect information and to **detain** suspected terrorists without having **warrants**. The number of terrorist attacks has somewhat decreased since the initiation of the war on terror. Nevertheless, critics contend that most terrorist groups are too **fragmented** and attacks too unpredictable to defend against fully. Because of this, many feel that anti-terrorism laws have simply given the government too much power to spy on ordinary citizens. **Words 416**

Reading Skill

The main idea of each paragraph gives a general idea that is explained in the rest of the paragraph.

- **Q** What is the main idea of paragraph 3?
- **A** While some significant terrorist attacks, such as those on September 11, 2001, are reported globally, most terrorist attacks go _____ by the majority of the global public.

Vocabulary in Context

A Match the words in bold from the passage with their correct definitions.

1. _____ broken into many pieces or groups

2. _____ to gradually cause someone to have a feeling or attitude

3. _____ a desire to help others without the hope of personal benefit

4. _____ affecting or harming many people without care or consideration

5. _____ to keep someone in a place, usually for questioning by the police

6. _____ a document given by a court to give the police power to do something

7. _____ referring to a person who feels he or she does not belong in a society

8. _____ having a strong belief that your opinions are right and others are wrong

B Look at the underlined words in the passage and choose the correct answers.

1. The word alarming in the first paragraph is closest in meaning to _____.
   a. aggressive   b. astonishing   c. distressing   d. expected

2. The word immediate in the second paragraph is closest in meaning to _____.
   a. particular   b. accidental   c. targeted   d. direct

3. The word hijack in the third paragraph is closest in meaning to _____.
   a. arrest   b. steal   c. explode   d. destroy

4. The word initiate in the fifth paragraph is closest in meaning to _____.
   a. begin   b. acquire   c. emerge   d. persist

C Choose the best word to complete each sentence.

1. In order to detain / retain your abilities, you must continually practice.

2. Natural disasters claim / contend the lives of thousands of people each year.

3. If you act respectably / respectively, people are more likely to treat you better.

Reading Comprehension

Main Idea

1. What is the passage mainly about?

   a. the deadliest terrorist attacks in modern history
   b. what terrorism is and how governments try to stop it
   c. reasons for the increase in terrorist attacks in recent years
   d. why fighting terrorism is more difficult than global conflicts

Details

2. What is the main purpose of terrorism?

   _____

3. Which of the following is true according to the passage?

   a. The country with the most terrorist attacks is Pakistan.
   b. Terrorists focus on major targets that will draw the most public attention.
   c. People who join terrorist groups believe that they create chaos in the world.
   d. A group of Israelis conducted an attack during the Munich Olympics in 1972.

4. What does the word **them** in the fourth paragraph refer to?

   a. terrorists
   b. lower social classes
   c. victims
   d. alienated groups

5. Which of the following is NOT true about terrorists?

   a. They are willing to sacrifice themselves to reach their goals.
   b. They generally come from groups that are not accepted by society.
   c. They believe that terrorism can correct the problems of the world.
   d. They usually want to gain wealth or power through terrorist acts.

6. What powers have government organizations received because of anti-terrorism laws?

   _____

Inference

7. What can be inferred from the passage?

   a. Most terrorist attacks have occurred in the U.S. and European countries.
   b. Most terrorist groups try to make their groups bigger to fight against their governments.
   c. The "war on terror" makes it possible for governments to defend against terrorism fully.
   d. Governments sometimes invade ordinary people's privacy to fight against terrorism.

Summary

A **Fill in the chart with the phrases in the box.**

	Terrorism, the New World War
Definition of Terrorism	Terrorism is the use of ❶_____ by non-government groups to ❷_____ among the public.
Terrorist Attacks	Some of the terrorist attacks, such as the September 11, 2001 attacks, are widely known, but tens of thousands more attacks ❸_____.
Recruiting Methods	• Terrorist groups will recruit members from alienated groups who are drawn by a ❹_____ to become terrorists. • Terrorists have a sense of ❺_____ to justify the violence they commit.
War on Terror	• The United States and other countries have started a "war on terror" to allow government organizations to ❻_____ on suspected terrorists. • While this has been somewhat effective, many feel that this has simply given governments too much power to spy on their citizens.

go unnoticed   collect data   indiscriminate violence
create fear   sense of altruism   self-righteous sacrifice

B **Complete the summary with correct words by referring to the chart above.**

❶_____ is a frightening form of warfare that can occur at almost any time. Terrorists will attack ❷_____ targets to draw the attention of the public. One such event was the murder of 11 Israelis at the 1972 Munich Olympics. Between 2000 to 2014, 140,000 people died in 61,000 acts of terrorism. The most significant was the September 11, 2001 attacks, but most attacks go ❸_____. Terrorist groups ❹_____ members from ❺_____ groups who become terrorists out of a sense of altruism. In response, the United States and other countries have initiated a "war on terror." While this has been somewhat ❻_____ in decreasing terrorist attacks, many feel that it has given governments too much ❼_____ to ❽_____ on citizens.

Unit 8

Theme | *Social Science*
Reading Skill | *Compare & Contrast*

What IQ and EQ Tests Actually Determine

Before You Read

A Think about the Topic

1. What do you think being "smart" means?
2. How accurate do you think intelligence tests are?

B Background Knowledge

The term IQ stands for intelligence quotient and was created by German psychologist William Stern in the early 1900s. Around this time, the French government approached psychologist Alfred Binet to create a test that could determine which schoolchildren would need extra learning assistance. He created a test that measured skills that are not specifically taught in schools, such as memory, attention, and problem-solving ability. Binet's test became widely used to measure the abilities of schoolchildren, military personnel, and even immigrants. Despite the popularity of the test, Binet cautioned that it could not measure all aspects of a person and that IQ can change over time. This has led to the development of another type of intelligence test, the EQ test.

Unit 8
Social Science | Compare & Contrast

What IQ and EQ Tests Actually Determine

▶ As you read, consider what intelligence quotient (IQ) and emotional intelligence quotient (EQ) tests measure.

Intelligence testing is based on the belief that a person's intelligence can be calculated and stated as an exact number by **administering** a series of standardized test questions. Such testing was first introduced in the mid-1800s by the British researcher Francis Galton. Since IQ tests were first given, methods used for measuring one's
5   intelligence **quotient** (IQ) have raised concerns among members of the scientific community. However, that has not limited their widespread popularity. In fact, IQ testing has also **spawned** the emotional intelligence quotient (EQ) test in an attempt to better predict a person's future success. Despite the **prevalence** of these tests, many psychologists still debate the **rationale** behind IQ and EQ testing.

10   Proponents of IQ testing argue that when properly administered, the results are accurate predictors of a person's academic ability. The basic **methodology**, which has remained unchanged since the test's creation, is to have the subject
15   answer two sections of questions. In the first, subjects are timed to see how quickly they answer a series of multiple choice questions. In the second, subjects are timed to see how quickly they can

recreate patterns, often an arrangement of blocks. Based on the times and the number of correct answers, the IQ, which is a fixed number, is calculated. More recent versions, such as the <mark>WISC-V</mark>, claim to be more accurate as they have more questions that measure a broader range of skills.

In contrast, EQ testing seeks to narrow down the range of subjects' abilities being tested. Individuals give responses to **hypothetical** situations. Points are allotted to how emotionally appropriate the given response is. This **assumes**, however, that people are answering honestly. The basis of the test is that people with greater emotional intelligence are better equipped to manage, perceive, and express emotions. This ability is why, advocates claim, people with a high EQ are more likely to be successful. As a result, some researchers propose adding classes to improve students' EQ.

Critics of these tests argue that both tests have serious flaws that render them useless. Considering that there is no consensus as to what constitutes intelligence, they claim all the tests are **invalid**. They also point to the fact that people's scores on the same subjects vary from test to test. Opponents also cite the biases in the tests as IQ test scores are **skewed** to favor those from specific social and cultural backgrounds. EQ tests can be "faked good," a term used to describe how test takers lie to raise their scores.

Words 416

Reading Skill

Comparing and contrasting is a way to explain how two or more things are similar and different.

Q   How do IQ and EQ tests differ in what they measure?
A   IQ tests have many question types to measure a _____ range of skills while EQ tests seek to _____ down the range of a subject's abilities.

Vocabulary in Context

A **Match the words in bold from the passage with their correct definitions.**

1. _____ not real but imaginary
2. _____ to create another similar thing
3. _____ to make something favor one group or result
4. _____ not correct or proper due to a flaw or error
5. _____ the state of being widely accepted or popular
6. _____ the degree of a characteristic in someone or something
7. _____ to believe something to be true without direct proof
8. _____ the process or method by which something such as a test is done

B **Look at the underlined words in the passage and choose the correct answers.**

1. The word administer in the first paragraph is closest in meaning to _____.
   a. supply   b. execute   c. distribute   d. observe

2. The word rationale in the first paragraph is closest in meaning to _____.
   a. reason   b. defense   c. appeal   d. proof

3. The word advocate in the third paragraph is closest in meaning to _____.
   a. interpreter   b. rival   c. protester   d. proponent

4. The word constitute in the fourth paragraph is closest in meaning to _____.
   a. comprise   b. permit   c. divide   d. accomplish

C **Choose the best word to complete each sentence.**

1. The movie was so popular that it spawned / skewed three sequels.

2. Her argument became valid / invalid after new evidence proved her wrong.

3. Opponents / Proponents of the city's bus plan say it will reduce traffic problems.

54

Reading Comprehension

Main Idea

1. **What is the passage mainly about?**

    a. a disagreement as to the use of a particular test

    b. the methods of measuring emotions and intellect

    c. the development of the intelligence of young children

    d. the potential harm in giving a numerical value to emotion

Details

2. **What are the types of questions on IQ tests?**

    _____

3. **Why does the author mention WISC-V?**

    a. to show that the future of IQ testing is promising

    b. to give an example of a test that cannot be "faked good"

    c. to give an example of a test that may yield better results

    d. to show that asking more questions is the key to measuring IQ

4. **Which of the following is NOT true according to the passage?**

    a. People's IQs can better determine their success than their EQs can.

    b. The WISC-V test includes a wider range of question types than older tests.

    c. Answering questions more quickly and accurately on tests shows a higher IQ.

    d. EQ test results are calculated based on the emotional appropriateness of responses.

5. **Why do some researchers want to add classes to schools that would benefit students' EQs?**

    _____

6. **Which of the following is true about IQ and EQ tests?**

    a. The tests are biased in favor of working class people.

    b. It is possible for people to lie on IQ tests to raise their scores.

    c. Older IQ tests were better at measuring people's emotional abilities.

    d. IQ cannot be measured since there is no agreement of what intelligence is.

Inference

7. **What can be inferred from the passage?**

    a. EQ tests have a longer history than IQ tests.

    b. More schools are introducing EQ classes into their curriculum.

    c. People who spend more time thinking would get a lower IQ score.

    d. Psychologists have become more skeptical of intelligence testing over time.

Summary

A Fill in the chart with the phrases in the box.

IQ Tests and EQ Tests	
IQ Tests	• IQ tests consist of two sets of questions measuring ability to answer multiple choice questions and to ❶_____. • Newer tests cover a broader range of skills which can be used to determine a person's exact intelligence.
EQ Tests	• EQ tests attempt to ❷_____ of the subjects' abilities being tested by asking them to answer questions about ❸_____. • People who give more emotionally appropriate answers are considered to have a better ability to ❹_____.
Criticisms	• One criticism is that there is no widely ❺_____ of what intelligence is. • The tests can be biased ❻_____ people from specific cultural and social groups.

accepted standard   recognize patterns   manage their emotions
in favor of   hypothetical situations   narrow down the range

B Complete the summary with correct words by referring to the chart above.

Intelligence tests use a series of standardized questions to determine a person's exact ❶_____ as an exact number. Supporters of IQ tests say that they are accurate predictors of a person's ❷_____ ability. Based on how ❸_____ and accurately subjects answer the questions on the test, their IQs can be calculated. While IQ tests attempt to measure a person's ❹_____ skill set, EQ tests attempt to ❺_____ down the range of the test taker's abilities being tested. Test takers are asked to give responses to a set of hypothetical situations to measure their ability to manage their ❻_____. Critics point out that such testing is flawed because there is no widely ❼_____ concept of intelligence and that the tests can be ❽_____ toward certain groups.

Unit 9

Theme | *Literature*
Reading Skill | *Main Idea*

The Different Forms of Satire

Before You Read

A Think about the Topic

1. What do you think satire refers to?
2. In what ways do you think you can experience satire?

B Background Knowledge

Some forms of media, such as news reports, are informative as they give facts and details about important events in the real world. Yet other kinds of media blend humor and information to provide commentary about the problems of society. This genre is satire, which has existed for thousands of years to make people laugh at the flaws of their society and its leaders but also to inspire change and to make the world a better place. Today, we can find satire in many forms of entertainment, such as plays, literature, television shows, and even music lyrics.

Unit 9
Literature | Main Idea

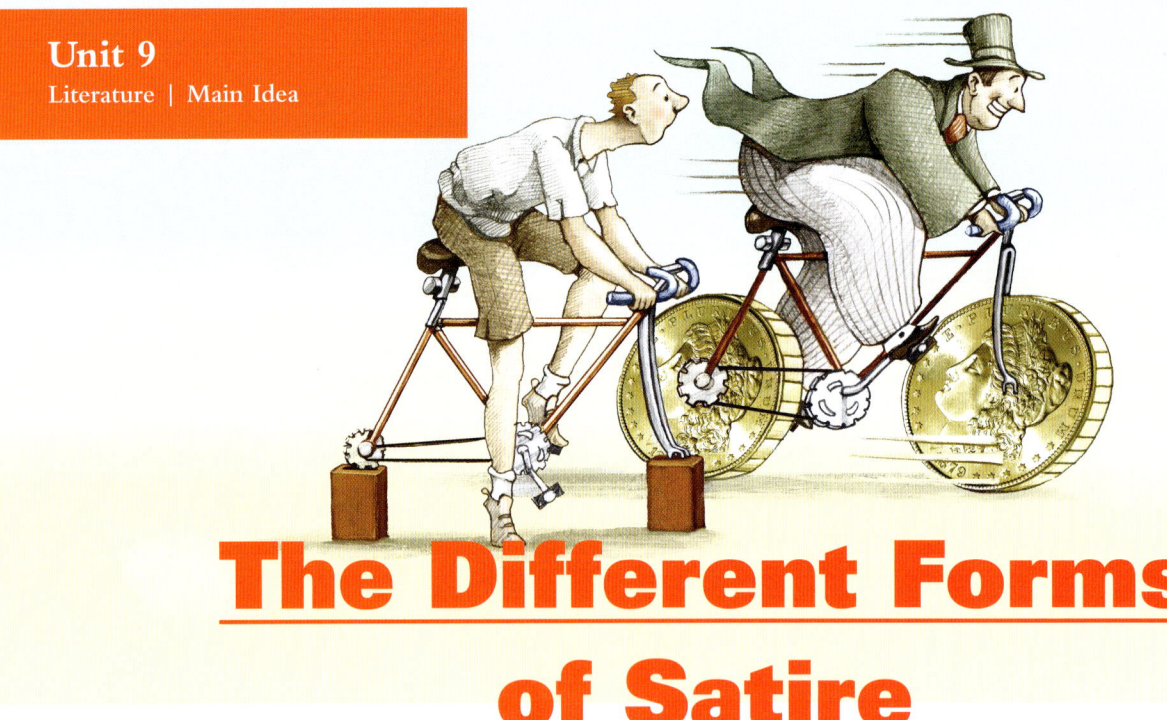

The Different Forms of Satire

▶ As you read, think about what the different targets of satirical works are.

Satire is a genre that uses **wit** to highlight the **folly**, greed, and narrow self-interests of people and society. Satire is at times funny, with irony and **sarcasm** important elements of it, but humor itself is not its purpose. Rather, its <u>aim</u> is to hold powerful persons and **institutions** up to ridicule in the hopes of changing and improving them. Consequently, most satire is political or social and offers a critical view of the people who shape society.

Many literary examples of satire exist throughout the ages. One of the oldest known works of satire is the Egyptian writing *The Satire of the Trades*. Ancient Greece and the Medieval Islamic world offer examples of satire. In these societies, satire was used, as it is now, to ridicule government officials into changing their policies, such as the plays of the ancient Greek writer Aristophanes.

A more <u>contemporary</u> example of satire is *Gulliver's Travels* by Irish author Jonathan Swift, which offered a satirical view of English society at that time. In the book, there are two political parties in the story distinguished by the size of their boot heels. This <u>inconsequential</u> difference between **them** was Swift's way of satirizing the minor disputes between the two rival political parties of his time. Another famous work of satire is Mark Twain's *The Adventures of Huckleberry Finn*. Written in 1884, just two decades after the American Civil War, the novel **mocks** the institution of slavery. One of the main characters in the story is Miss Watson, who owns a slave, Jim, even though she considers herself a "good Christian woman" with strong values. Twain uses satire to show the **hypocrisy** of her owning a slave even though she is a Christian.

The genre of satire is not limited to literature. Many hugely popular television shows, programs, and events use satire as a form of social commentary. These include comedy programs such as *Saturday Night Live*, which uses satire to point out the flaws and peculiar habits of celebrities through its comedic **skits**. The long-running animated television series *The Simpsons* is also satirical. It has a large cast of strange characters that are used to make fun of different parts of American culture. The show addresses issues relating to education, **gender equality**, class divisions, and the media. The Ig Nobel Prizes are awards given to recognize unusual scientific achievements. Although they satirize the Nobel Prizes, their stated purpose is to "honor achievements that make people laugh, and then make them think." **Words 415**

▲ The Simpsons

Reading Skill

The main idea is usually at the beginning of a text and makes a general statement.

Q What is the main idea of the passage?
A Different _____ of satire have been used throughout history to ridicule people and institutions in _____ in the hope of changing them.

Vocabulary in Context

A Match the words or phrases in bold from the passage with their correct definitions.

1. _____ foolish or illogical behavior
2. _____ a short comedic performance
3. _____ the intelligent use of language for humorous effect
4. _____ to criticize someone in a humorous but mean way
5. _____ a custom or practice that has existed for a long time
6. _____ the idea that men and women should be treated equally
7. _____ behavior that does not match with what someone claims to believe
8. _____ the use of words that are the opposite of what you mean to insult someone

B Look at the underlined words in the passage and choose the correct answers.

1. The word aim in the first paragraph is closest in meaning to _____.
   a. goal   b. ambition   c. direction   d. audience

2. The word contemporary in the third paragraph is closest in meaning to _____.
   a. controversial   b. popular   c. modern   d. temporary

3. The word inconsequential in the third paragraph is closest in meaning to _____.
   a. opposite   b. insignificant   c. ineffective   d. inseparable

4. The word peculiar in the fourth paragraph is closest in meaning to _____.
   a. ordinary   b. particular   c. intense   d. unusual

C Choose the best word to complete each sentence.

1. The number of literary / literate people in the country is low due to the poor education system.

2. She was given an award in recognition of her many achievements / improvements in science.

3. In developed countries, the institution / organization of arranged marriages was no longer maintained in the 20th century.

Reading Comprehension

Main Idea

1 **What is the passage mainly about?**

   a. examples of satire successfully changing society

   b. a comparison of satire across different forms of media

   c. the use of satire to mock political leaders and celebrities

   d. a definition of satire and examples of it throughout the ages

Details

2 **According to the passage, which of the following is true about satire?**

   a. The use of irony and sarcasm is its most important elements.

   b. It attempts to reform society by mocking people in power.

   c. Satire used in other forms of media mainly focuses on criticizing politicians.

   d. The purpose of satire used in literature is different from that of other forms of media.

3 **What does the word them in the third paragraph refer to?**

   a. boot heels

   b. political parties in the story

   c. minor disputes

   d. political parties of his time

4 **What is Miss Watson's hypocrisy in *The Adventures of Huckleberry Finn*?**

   _____

5 **In paragraphs 2 and 3, the author states that** _____.

   a. the purpose of satire has not changed over time

   b. Irish politicians argued about the size of their boot heels

   c. Americans who were Christians were against the institution of slavery

   d. the satire in *Gulliver's Travels* is more critical than that in *The Adventures of Huckleberry Finn*

6 **What are the targets of satire in *Saturday Night Live* and *The Simpsons*?**

   _____

Inference

7 **What CANNOT be inferred from the passage?**

   a. A wide range of social issues is targeted by satire.

   b. There has been injustice in society since ancient times.

   c. Satire usually has a deeper meaning beyond its humor.

   d. The humorous aspects of satire have gained more importance in recent years.

Unit 9   61

Summary

A Fill in the chart with the phrases in the box.

The Different Forms of Satire	
Definition of Satire	• Satire is a genre that uses wit to ❶_____ and self-interests of people and society. • Its aim is to ridicule powerful people and institutions to ❷_____.
Satire in Literature	• Ancient Greece and Medieval Islamic societies used satire to ridicule government officials. • *Gulliver's Travels* by Jonathan Swift satirizes the ❸_____ between British political parties of Swift's era. • Mark Twain's *The Adventures of Huckleberry Finn* used satire to criticize Christians for ❹_____.
Satire in Other Media	• The television programs *Saturday Night Live* and *The Simpsons* use satire to make fun of the ❺_____ and American culture. • The Ig Nobel Prizes satirize the Nobel Prizes, and they seek to ❻_____ and then think.

> change them   owning slaves   highlight the folly
> make people laugh   minor disputes   peculiarities of celebrities

B Complete the summary with correct words by referring to the chart above.

Satire is a genre which uses ❶_____ to highlight the folly and self-interests of people. By ridiculing those in ❷_____, satire aims to change these people and ❸_____. Literary satire has existed throughout the ages. Ancient Greek and Medieval Islamic writers used it to ❹_____ government officials. More recent examples include *The Adventures of Huckleberry Finn* by Mark Twain, which criticized Christians for owning ❺_____, and Jonathan Swift's *Gulliver's Travels*, which humorously critiqued the minor disputes between ❻_____ parties of that era. Satire is also present in other forms of ❼_____, such as the television programs *Saturday Night Live* and *The Simpsons*. The Ig Nobel Prizes ❽_____ the Nobel Prizes to make people laugh and then think.

Unit 10

Theme | *Sociology*
Reading Skill | *Categorizing*

Natural Factors Influencing Development

Before You Read

A   Think about the Topic

1. Why can people live better lives when their nations are wealthier?
2. How do you think geography affects a nation's development?

B   Background Knowledge

Many factors enable a nation to develop and become wealthy. Having a large enough population is one factor as there need to be people who can work in jobs. Stable political and legal systems are also important. Governments must be willing and able to maintain an orderly society that will allow for the development of the infrastructure that businesses need to grow. Related to this is providing a well-funded and rigorous education system to prepare citizens for jobs requiring advanced skills. As much as these factors matter, no country can develop easily if its natural environment is poor. Countries in poor locations or with few resources struggle to become wealthy.

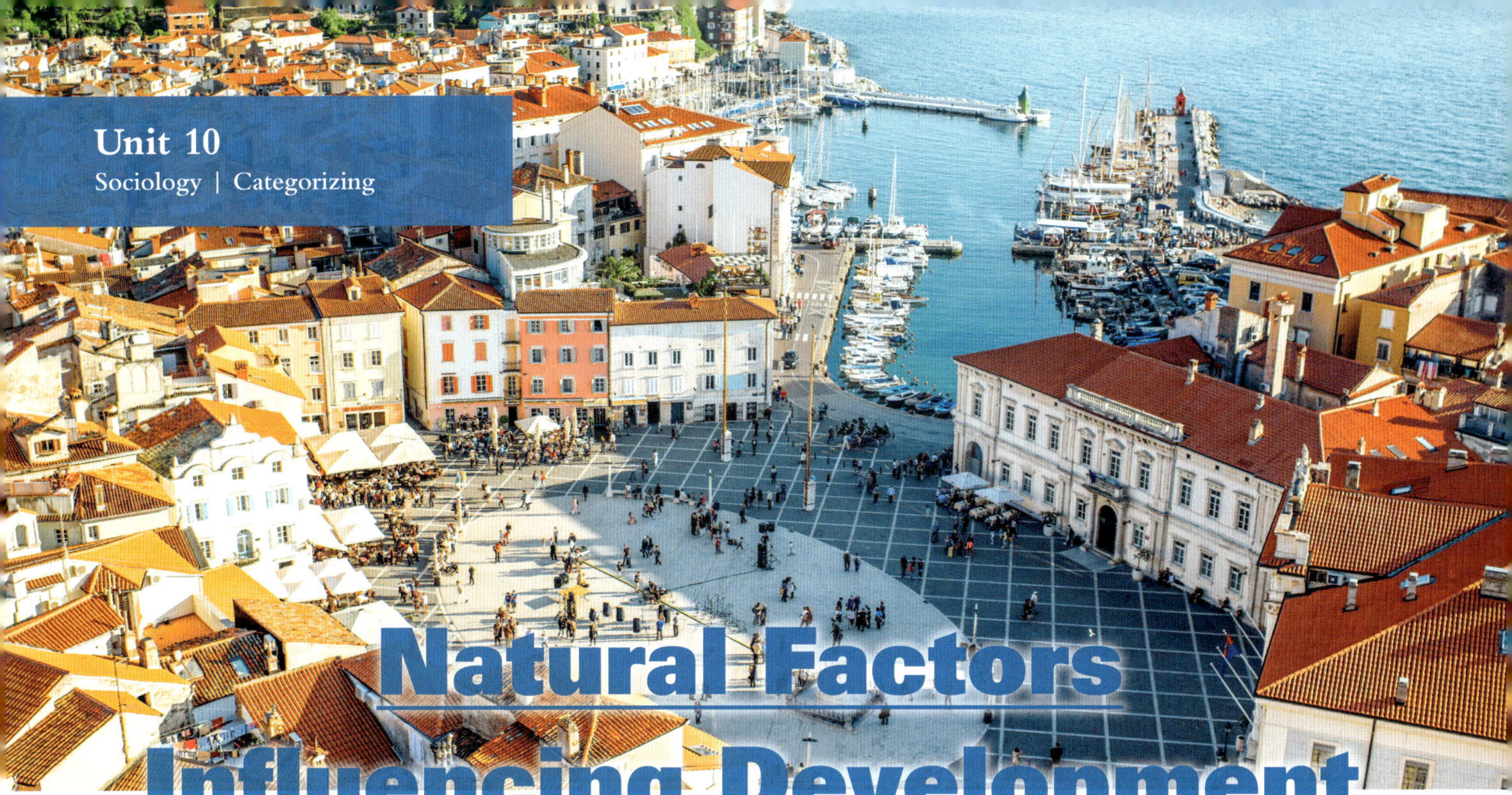

Unit 10
Sociology | Categorizing

Natural Factors Influencing Development

▶ *As you read, pay attention to the three main natural factors that affect how wealthy a nation is.*

It is well-known that some countries are far wealthier than others. Some contend that poor countries remain impoverished because they are **exploited** by the wealthy nations of the world. Others argue that these poor nations are corrupt and deserve to remain in **squalor**. Although there is some merit to these arguments, natural factors often have an even greater effect on the economies of these nations than either of these elements.

Perhaps the most critical factor in a nation's development is its geography. It is not a coincidence that many of the world's poorest nations are located in **tropical** regions near the equator, where the weather is hot, the land less fertile, and water scarce. Thus, companies do not invest in these countries because they would spend too much money on electricity and other resources to make significant profit. Conversely, countries located in more **temperate** regions, such as the United States and many European countries, have had a naturally easier time developing. These places have huge tracts of fertile land, moderate temperatures, and a good amount of rainfall. Due to these factors, companies are more likely to open businesses in such nations since they would have to invest far less time and energy to flourish.

In addition to geography, a country's location also plays a major role in its development. The great empires of the world have always had access to maritime trade routes, and this rule still applies to generating national wealth. Many of the world's poorest nations are **hindered** by being **landlocked** or mountainous and do not have navigable rivers or access to harbors. On the contrary, China and the United States, the two largest economies in the world, are home to some of the world's busiest ports. This affords them access to global shipping lanes, making it easy for <mark>them</mark> to export their products all over the world at a low cost.

A third factor is natural resources. To generate wealth, countries must be able to exploit their resources. For instance, countries in the Middle East have one of the most precious natural resources: oil. They have developed the infrastructure necessary to extract and distribute their vast oil **reserves** to become wealthy. South American countries have been able to manage their **renewable** resources—timber and rubber—to enable them to develop their economies. Some nations rich in resources, such as Ghana, Tanzania, and Venezuela, remain poor. However, countries that lack appreciable natural resources are at a major economic disadvantage.   **Words 411**

Rubber extration ▶

Reading Skill

Categorizing information means to arrange information or items into different groups.

Q What are the three natural factors that influence the economies of nations?

A The three factors are _____, location, and _____.

Vocabulary in Context

A Match the words in bold from the passage with their correct definitions.

1. _____ able to be used over and over

2. _____ to treat unfairly or take advantage of

3. _____ not too hot or too cold; moderate

4. _____ surrounded by land with no coast

5. _____ very bad or unpleasant conditions

6. _____ a supply of something not needed immediately

7. _____ describing areas with warm climates near the equator

8. _____ to slow down the process of the development of something

B Look at the underlined words in the passage and choose the correct answers.

1. The word merit in the first paragraph is closest in meaning to _____.
   a. capability   b. doubt   c. worth   d. disadvantage

2. The word critical in the second paragraph is closest in meaning to _____.
   a. significant   b. broad   c. considerate   d. harmful

3. The word afford in the third paragraph is closest in meaning to _____.
   a. reserve   b. guarantee   c. enhance   d. offer

4. The word appreciable in the fourth paragraph is closest in meaning to _____.
   a. adequate   b. substantial   c. distinct   d. relevant

C Choose the best word to complete each sentence.

1. The company had to pay a fine for exploiting / exploring its workers.

2. Although he is an excellent athlete, he is very moderate / modest about his accomplishments.

3. There has been no appreciable / comparable change in his behavior after being punished.

Reading Comprehension

Main Idea

1 **What is the passage mainly about?**

   a. the importance of natural conditions in a country's development
   b. countries that have poor environments yet still become wealthy
   c. factors that companies consider before choosing a country to invest in
   d. historical factors that have allowed certain countries to develop more rapidly

Details

2 **According to the passage, why do companies not want to invest in tropical regions?**

   a. These areas do not have access to harbors and navigable rivers.
   b. These regions have excessive amounts of rainfall during certain seasons.
   c. Companies would spend too much money on resources such as electricity.
   d. Governments in tropical areas are often corrupt and do not support businesses.

3 **What geographic factors do the United States and Europe have that helped them develop?**

   _____

4 **What does the word them in the third paragraph refer to?**

   a. global shipping lanes   b. landlocked nations
   c. world's busiest ports   d. China and the United States

5 **Why are countries that have access to oceans and rivers wealthier than landlocked countries?**

   _____

6 **In paragraph 4, the author states that** _____.

   a. infrastructure is crucial for exploiting natural resources
   b. countries with large amounts of natural resources are always wealthy
   c. nations with appreciable amounts of renewable resources developed quickly
   d. the majority of South American countries gained wealth from timber and rubber

Inference

7 **What can be inferred from the passage?**

   a. Highly developed countries are likely to have busy shipping ports.
   b. Sending products by sea is more expensive than shipping them over land.
   c. Farming companies are generally found in countries located in tropical areas.
   d. It is necessary for a country to use its renewable resources to become wealthy.

Summary

A Fill in the chart with the phrases in the box.

Natural Factors Influencing Development	
Geography and Climate	• Nations with ❶_____ are usually poor because businesses will have to spend too much money on resources to make enough profit. • In temperate regions, businesses would have to invest ❷_____ and energy to flourish there.
Location	• Countries that are ❸_____ have a hard time shipping their products cheaply and easily. • Some wealthy nations, such as the USA and China, have access to global ❹_____, so they can distribute their products all over the world.
Natural Resources	• Countries in the Middle East have large quantities of oil while South American countries have ❺_____ supplies that they can use to develop their economies. • Nations that do not have access to natural resources are at a major ❻_____.

shipping routes   timber and rubber   tropical climates
less money   economic disadvantage   landlocked or mountainous

B Complete the summary with correct words by referring to the chart above.

Many ❶_____ factors influence the development of a nation. A nation's geography and ❷_____ are perhaps the most important. Nations in tropical regions are poor because companies will not ❸_____ in the region since they will not make enough profit. In contrast, companies will open businesses in ❹_____ regions since it requires less money to flourish there. A country's ❺_____ also matters a lot. Many poor nations are landlocked or mountainous, so they cannot ❻_____ their products easily or cheaply. The final factor is natural resources. Middle Eastern countries, for instance, have ❼_____ to large quantities of oil while South American countries have vast amounts of timber and rubber. When countries lack such resources, they are at a major economic ❽_____.

Unit 11

Theme | *Biology*
Reading Skill | *Main Idea of Each Paragraph*

The Eurasian Eagle-Owl

Before You Read

A Think about the Topic

1. What are some animals that are major predators?
2. How do you think most birds get their food?

B Background Knowledge

Gray wolves, lions, killer whales, and crocodiles: what do these animals have in common? They are all well-known predators. These hunters use their size, speed, and power to take down other animals to get their next meal. As human beings, we respect and fear these animals for their hunting abilities. However, not all predators can be found on land or underwater; some of the most dangerous hunters live in the skies. One such predator is the Eurasian eagle-owl. This bird, with its huge size and sharp claws, attacks a number of animals, some of them much larger than itself. Although the eagle-owl is a powerful predator, it may need the help of human beings to survive.

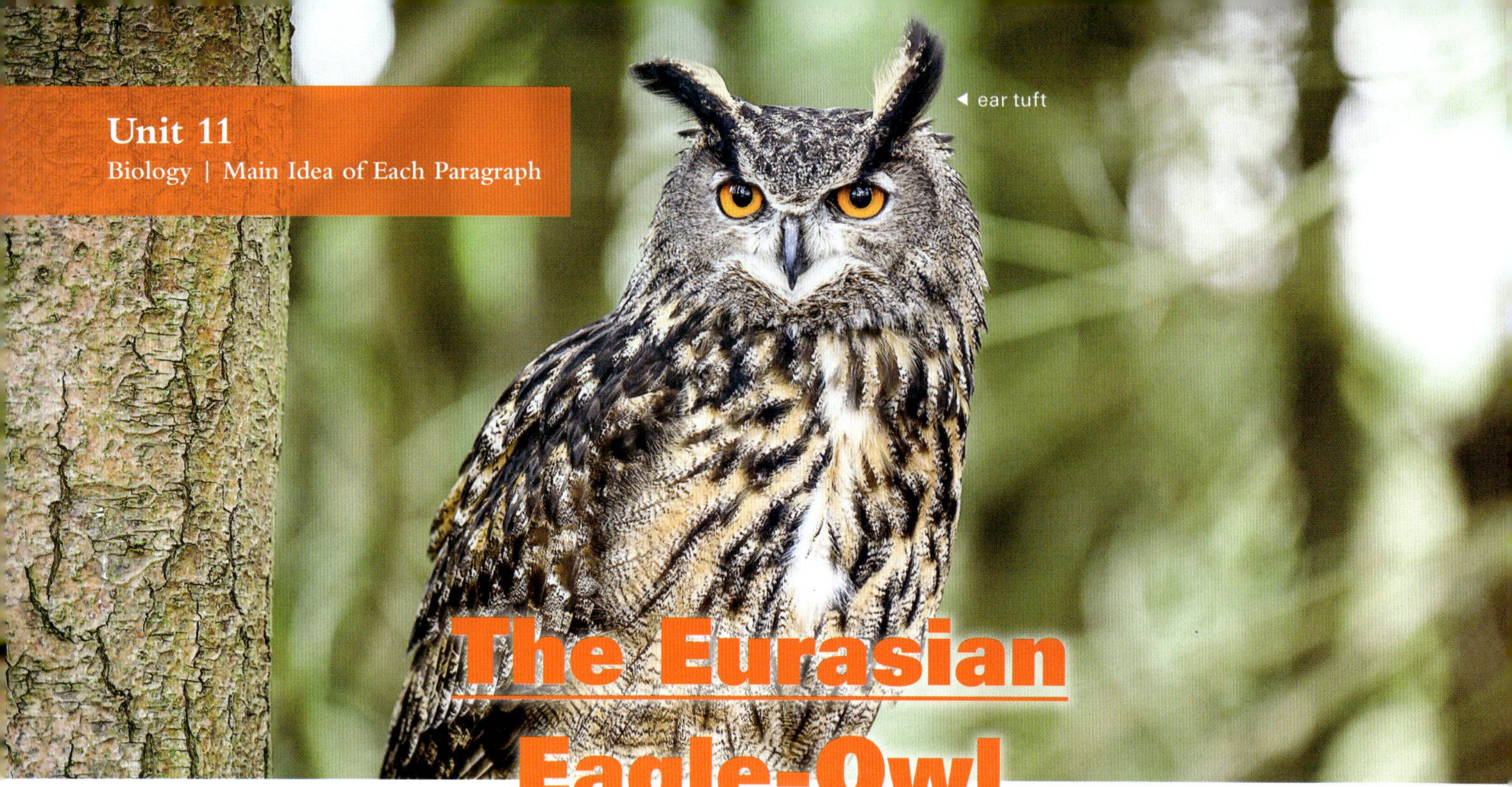

Unit 11
Biology | Main Idea of Each Paragraph

◀ ear tuft

The Eurasian Eagle-Owl

▶ As you read, consider the traits of the eagle-owl that make it a powerful predator.

One of the most striking **birds of prey** is the Eurasian eagle-owl. This bird has distinctive *ear tufts, orange eyes, and sharp claws, but it stands out mainly due to its sheer size. The eagle-owl is one of the largest birds in the world. Adult females grow up to 75 centimeters in length, have a wingspan of nearly two meters, and weigh as much as 4.5 kilograms, with adult males being slightly smaller.

Due to its formidable size, the eagle-owl sits atop the food chain. It is an opportunistic hunter that will attempt to catch any prey of suitable size. Its most common prey consists of small mammals such as mice and rabbits, but it is also known to hunt other birds, mainly pigeons. Some eagle-owls have been seen capturing adult roe deer weighing up to 17 kilograms, making them by far the largest prey animal of any bird. The eagle-owl prefers to hunt at night, resting on **perches** or flying at low altitudes to look for its next meal. Thanks to its keen eyesight and hearing abilities, the eagle-owl can detect even the slightest sounds and movements, enabling it to catch its prey highly effectively.

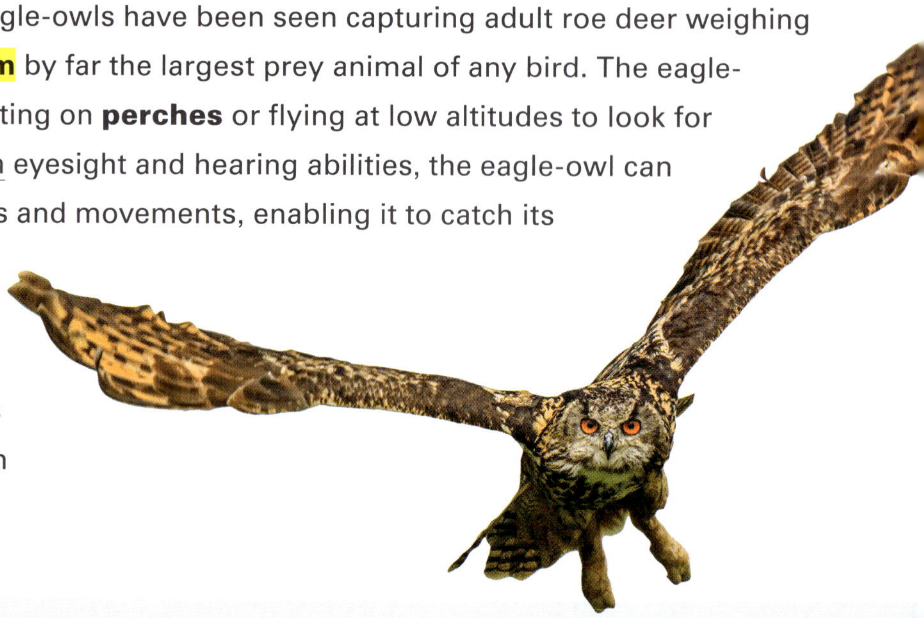

This capable hunter is found throughout many parts of Asia and Europe, as well as in

North Africa. It is suited to live in many habitats, preferring to **dwell** in areas with rocky formations and cliffs, including the Himalayas and the Alps, as well as wooded habitats and **marshes**. These environments give it many high areas from which to **perch** so that it can safely search for prey animals below. However, it is also known to live in open areas such as farmlands and grasslands which allow it to <u>monitor</u> large areas at once, helping it to find food more quickly.

As human **settlements encroach** upon eagle-owl territories in Western Europe, the mortality rate of these <u>majestic</u> creatures has increased, with many of them dying from **electrocution** or flying into electrical towers. Therefore, governments and other organizations have been **reintroducing** the bird since the 1970s. Perhaps the most prominent example of this occurred from the 1970s to the 1990s in Belgium and Luxembourg, where 1,000 of the birds were reintroduced into nature. Studies have shown that this program was successful as the birds were able to breed at rates similar to wild eagle-owls. **Words 389**

*ear tuft: long feathers above the eyes of owls and other birds that look like ears but are not

Reading Skill

The main idea of each paragraph gives a general idea that is explained in the rest of the paragraph.

Q   What is the main idea of paragraph 4?
A   The spread of human _____ has caused the number of eagle-owl deaths to _____.

Vocabulary in Context

A Match the words or phrases in bold from the passage with their correct definitions.

1. _____ to live in a place

2. _____ a place where people have come to live

3. _____ a bird that hunts small animals for food

4. _____ an area of wet land that is soft and has a lot of grass

5. _____ to bring back to a previous state or place; to restore

6. _____ to move into an area gradually that is outside normal limits

7. _____ to sit on something high above the ground; a place where a bird sits

8. _____ the state of being shocked or killed by a large amount of electricity

B Look at the underlined words in the passage and choose the correct answers.

1. The word sheer in the first paragraph is closest in meaning to _____.
   a. vertical   b. absolute   c. moderate   d. transparent

2. The word keen in the second paragraph is closest in meaning to _____.
   a. striking   b. significant   c. anxious   d. acute

3. The word monitor in the third paragraph is closest in meaning to _____.
   a. maintain   b. display   c. observe   d. ensure

4. The word majestic in the fourth paragraph is closest in meaning to _____.
   a. grand   b. humble   c. respectable   d. complicated

C Choose the best word or phrase to complete each sentence.

1. Andrew is the most capable / available basketball player on our team.

2. Although the shark is a dangerous prey / predator , it rarely attacks human beings.

3. Promotions from companies have to stand out / stand for to attract customers' attention.

Reading Comprehension

Main Idea

1. **What is the passage mainly about?**

   a. animals that are commonly hunted by eagle-owls

   b. reasons that eagle-owl populations are decreasing

   c. a bird that is notable for its impressive size and hunting abilities

   d. a type of animal that has become a threat to human settlements

Details

2. **What does the word them in the second paragraph refer to?**

   a. roe deer   b. eagle-owls   c. pigeons   d. small mammals

3. **What characteristics allow the eagle-owl to catch its prey efficiently?**

   _____

4. **Which of the following is NOT true according to the passage?**

   a. Female eagle-owls are larger in size than male eagle-owls.

   b. Eagle-owls most often catch mice and other small mammals.

   c. It is more difficult for eagle-owls to catch prey in grasslands.

   d. The growth of human settlements has led to more eagle-owl deaths.

5. **Why do eagle-owls frequently live in areas with rocky formations?**

   _____

6. **What does the author mention in paragraph 4?**

   a. The majority of eagle-owls have died from being hunted.

   b. Efforts to preserve the eagle-owl only began in the past decade.

   c. Eagle-owls brought into nature by humans have been able to reproduce naturally.

   d. Eagle-owls in nature have longer lifespans because of government programs to protect them.

Inference

7. **What can be inferred from the passage?**

   a. It is common for birds to hunt big mammals as the eagle-owl does.

   b. It is possible for the eagle-owl to thrive in a variety of environments.

   c. Eagle-owls can only live in areas with high populations of small mammals.

   d. Eagle-owls are mostly active during the daylight hours rather than at night.

Summary

A Fill in the chart with the phrases in the box.

	The Eurasian Eagle-Owl
Hunting	• The bird sits at the top of the ❶_____ due to its formidable size. • It generally catches ❷_____ and other birds, but some eagle-owls have been observed catching adult roe deer. • It generally hunts at night.
Habitat	• The eagle-owl most typically lives in Asia, Europe, and North Africa. • It dwells in several types of areas such as ❸_____ as well as marshes and grasslands.
Conservation	• The encroachment of ❹_____ has caused the ❺_____ of these birds to increase. • Governments in Europe have undertaken efforts to ❻_____, with the most successful instance occurring in a program in Belgium and Luxembourg.

| rocky cliffs | food chain | human settlements |
| mortality rate | small mammals | reintroduce the bird |

B Complete the summary with correct words by referring to the chart above.

The Eurasian eagle-owl is one of the ❶_____ birds in the world, sitting at the ❷_____ of the food chain. As an opportunistic ❸_____, it generally catches small mammals and other birds. Eagle-owls have even been seen catching roe deer that weigh 17 kilograms. The eagle-owl prefers hunting at ❹_____ while perching high above the ground to find its next meal. Eagle-owls are commonly found in Asia, Europe and North Africa, dwelling in a variety of habitats such as ❺_____ cliffs as well as marshes and grasslands. Due to the ❻_____ of human settlements, the ❼_____ rate of these birds has increased. For this reason, European governments have been ❽_____ the bird, with the most successful case happening in Belgium and Luxembourg.

Unit 12

Theme | *People*
Reading Skill | *Cause & Effect*

The Works of Louis Pasteur

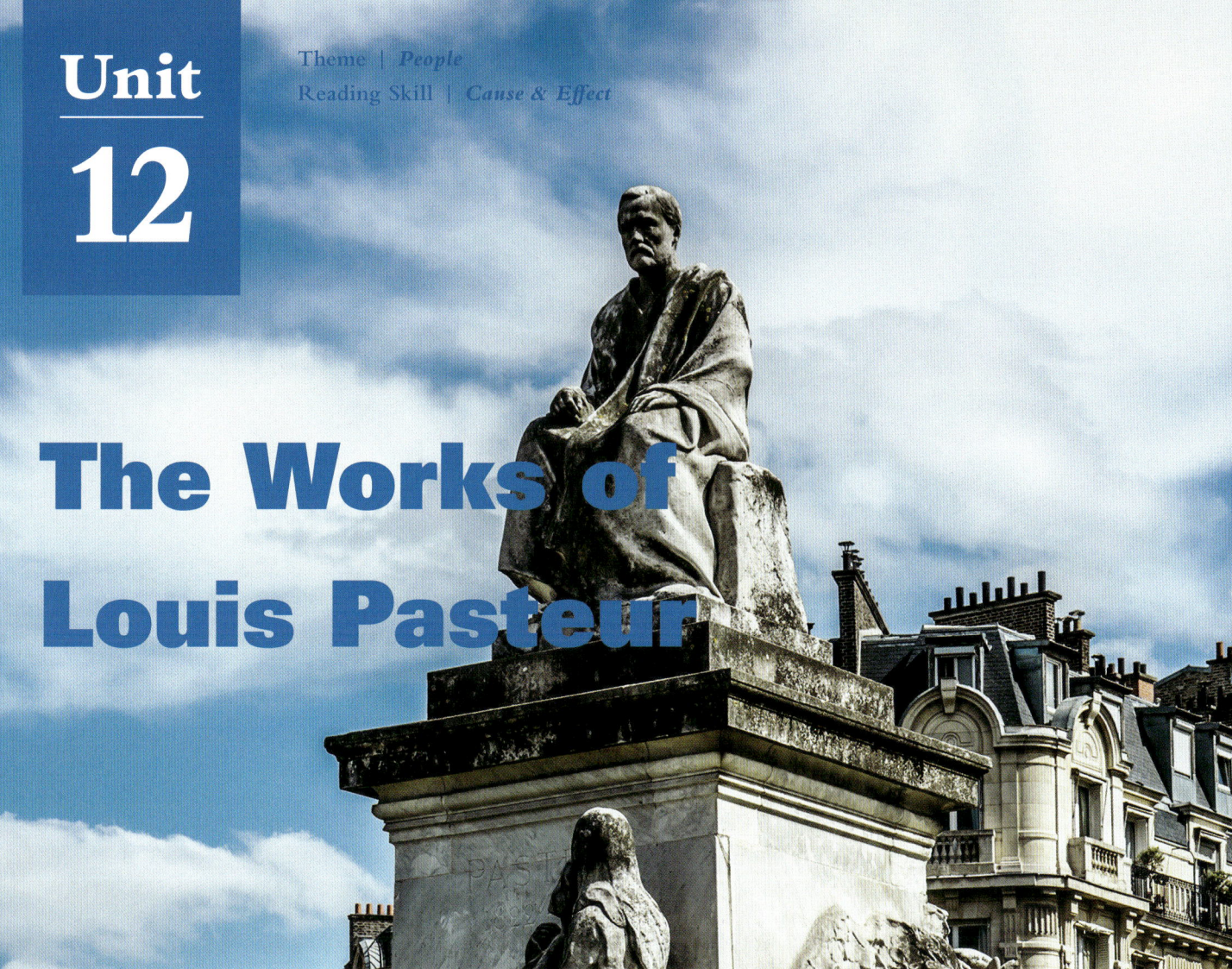

Before You Read

A Think about the Topic

1. Is it possible for something good to come from a mistake?
2. Why do you think you should wash your hands after using the bathroom?

B Background Knowledge

Fermentation is the process in which yeast turns sugars into ethanol, a type of alcohol, and carbon dioxide. Sugars from fruits, vegetables, grains, etc. can be broken down and turned into simpler forms of alcohol and carbon dioxide. Fermentation is used in many drinks and foods around the world. Wines and champagnes are products produced when yeast breaks down the sugars in grapes. Certain foods can also be fermented. Some foods, such as kimchi, are fermented not only to develop their unique taste but also to preserve the vegetables long after the end of the harvest. In other cultures, fish and meats are fermented for similar reasons.

Unit 12
People | Cause & Effect

The Works of Louis Pasteur

▶ *While you read, pay attention to how Louis Pasteur's discoveries helped to save people's lives.*

Louis Pasteur has long been considered a giant in the development of modern science. Born in France to a *tanner, Pasteur attended the prestigious Ecole Normale Superieure, an institution of higher education in Paris. During his time there, he began working with organic molecules. This work would later prove **instrumental** in his discoveries that would save millions of lives around the world.

His first work was with winemakers who had difficulty consistently producing quality alcohol. Normally, the process of fermentation converts the sugar from the grapes into alcohol. However, for these winemakers, sour *lactic acid was sometimes produced instead, ruining the entire mixture. It was known that yeast was present in the mix, and its presence was **attributed to** spontaneous generation. Pasteur disproved this idea with his "germ theory," in which he argued that microbes in the air contaminate food and cause yeast and other types of fungus to grow. Based on this theory, Pasteur proved that another microbe was using the sugar that the yeast needed to make alcohol. That was what was responsible for the spoilage of French wine. To keep this from happening, he boiled a vat of grape juice to 55

degrees Celsius, which **sterilized** it without ruining the taste. He then reintroduced yeast, ensuring that no other bacteria contaminated the mixture. This process came to be known as pasteurization, which saved France's wine industry and ensured Pasteur's fame.

A more important aspect of this work is that it suggested that foreign bacteria could have **deleterious** effects. In response, a few doctors began experimenting with sterilizing equipment and operating surfaces. Previously, few doctors would even wash their hands as they moved from patient to patient. The results were dramatic as the number of post-operative infections, which were frequently more lethal than the surgeries, plummeted. **Seizing upon** this **validation** of his work, Pasteur sought additional ways to prevent bacterial, or germ, infections.

His greatest discovery was **serendipitous**. Upon leaving a plate of bacteria out too long, he killed it. Deciding not to waste it, he tried injecting healthy chickens with the germs. Not only did the chickens not become ill, but they also gained **immunity** to the disease. The use of vaccines was not new as the English physician Edward Jenner had previously discovered a vaccination to prevent smallpox. Pasteur's work was so monumental because he was able to create vaccines artificially. This enabled scientists to protect people from a number of dangerous and potentially life-threatening pathogens. In time, a number of them would be nearly completely eradicated.   **Words 421**

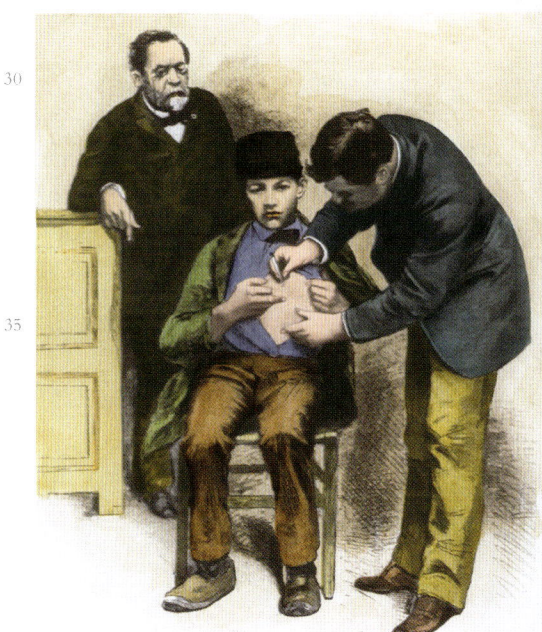

* tanner: a person who turns animal skins into leather
* lactic acid: a chemical that exists in sour milk and is produced by your body when you exercise

Reading Skill

Cause and effect is when one event causes something to happen. The cause explains why something happens, and the effect is what happens as a result.

Q   Why was lactic acid produced in some mixtures of wine?

A   Another _____ used the sugar that the yeast needed to make alcohol.

Vocabulary in Context

A **Match the words or phrases in bold from the passage with their correct definitions.**

1. _____ damaging or harmful

2. _____ to take advantage of something quickly

3. _____ proof that something is true or correct

4. _____ very important in causing something to happen

5. _____ to say that something is the result of something else

6. _____ lucky in finding something beneficial by accident or chance

7. _____ the power to keep yourself from being infected by a disease

8. _____ to clean something by removing all the germs or bacteria

B **Look at the underlined words in the passage and choose the correct answers.**

1. The word prestigious in the first paragraph is closest in meaning to _____.
   a. dominant   b. famous   c. respected   d. minor

2. The word consistently in the second paragraph is closest in meaning to _____.
   a. steadily   b. constructively   c. inexpensively   d. occasionally

3. The word lethal in the third paragraph is closest in meaning to _____.
   a. risky   b. vulnerable   c. beneficial   d. deadly

4. The word monumental in the fourth paragraph is closest in meaning to _____.
   a. efficient   b. discouraging   c. tremendous   d. discrete

C **Choose the best word to complete each sentence.**

1. You shouldn't eat food that has been sitting out too long since it can be contaminated / corrupted.

2. Many famous inventions were serendipitous / deliberate discoveries that nobody expected.

3. Our company does not produce these phones but simply attributes / distributes them globally.

Reading Comprehension

Main Idea

1 **What is the passage mainly about?**

   a. the effects of the work of a French scientist and its lasting consequences
   b. the complicated methods that allowed Pasteur to achieve amazing success
   c. how science frequently relies on accidental occurrences to solve great problems
   d. the problems faced by early scientists and doctors regarding norms of cleanliness

Details

2 **Why was there some inconsistency in early wine production?**

   _____

3 **What does the word it in the second paragraph refer to?**

   a. microbe   b. yeast   c. alcohol   d. grape juice

4 **Which of the following is NOT true according to the passage?**

   a. Pasteur added yeast to grape juice after sterilizing it with heat.
   b. Pasteur's germ theory proved that microbes in the air contaminate food.
   c. The first vaccines were developed as a result of Pasteur's experiments.
   d. More people died from infections after surgeries than from the surgeries themselves.

5 **According to paragraph 4, which is true about Pasteur's method of discovering artificial vaccines?**

   a. It had much more to do with luck than methodology.
   b. It came about after he got the idea to vaccinate chickens.
   c. It is only of limited use and is also very hard to duplicate.
   d. It showed no scientific creativity and was only a minor discovery.

6 **What was the long-term effect of Pasteur's discovery of artificial vaccinations?**

   It resulted in the _____ of many potentially _____.

Inference

7 **What CANNOT be inferred from the passage?**

   a. Many of Pasteur's discoveries are still being used today.
   b. Heating grape juice to over 55 degrees Celsius spoils the taste of wine.
   c. The French wine industry suffered economic losses before using pasteurization.
   d. Doctors were aware of the danger of foreign microbes prior to Pasteur's work.

Summary

A Fill in the chart with the phrases in the box.

The Works of Louis Pasteur	
Germ Theory and Pasteurization	• Pasteur worked with winemakers to help them prevent their wine ❶_____. • He developed the concept of germ theory to prove that microbes were ❷_____. • To prevent this, Pasteur heated the wine to 55 degrees Celsius to sterilize it in a process known as pasteurization.
Sterilization of Equipment	• Pasteur suggested that bacteria on medical equipment and operating surfaces ❸_____. • Sterilization caused the number of post-operative infections to ❹_____.
Discovery of Vaccination	• By accidentally leaving out a plate of bacteria, Pasteur discovered that chickens injected with the dead bacteria became ❺_____ the disease caused by the bacteria. • This discovery led to the creation of ❻_____, which protected many people from potentially deadly diseases.

immune to   artificial vaccinations   caused infections
decrease sharply   from spoiling   contaminating the wine

B Complete the summary with correct words by referring to the chart above.

French scientist Louis Pasteur made numerous scientific ❶_____ that saved the lives of millions of people across the world. His first work was helping French winemakers stop their wine from ❷_____. He developed ❸_____ theory to explain that a microbe ❹_____ the wine and produced lactic acid. Heating the wine to the right temperature kills the microbes and preserves the wine. This process became known as pasteurization. Pasteur also explained that foreign bacteria could cause lethal ❺_____, so some doctors began to ❻_____ their equipment and operating surfaces. Later, Pasteur made the discovery that dead bacteria may be used as a vaccine against ❼_____. This enabled scientists to create ❽_____ vaccinations, which saved the lives of millions of people.

Unit 13

Theme | *Geology*
Reading Skill | *Main Idea & Details*

The Difficulty of Predicting Earthquakes

Before You Read

A Think about the Topic

1. What do you think the most dangerous types of natural disasters are?
2. How do you think scientists can predict when an earthquake can happen?

B Background Knowledge

Natural disasters come in many forms. Among the most dangerous types of natural disasters are floods. These huge flows of water can overwhelm our defenses and destroy communities in a very short time. For instance, the 1931 floods in China killed an estimated one to four million people. Hurricanes and typhoons are other disasters that can lead to major damage and thousands of deaths. The Bhola cyclone that hit Bangladesh in 1970 may have resulted in as many as half a million deaths. As frightening as these disasters are, perhaps earthquakes are the deadliest type of natural disaster. These violent ground movements can occur at almost any time without warning, and therefore scientists must work to predict them more accurately.

Unit 13
Geology | Main Idea & Details

The Difficulty of Predicting Earthquakes

▶ As you read, pay attention to the factors that make it so difficult to anticipate the next earthquake.

Earthquakes are perhaps the deadliest type of natural disaster. These ground **tremors** can cause landslides and tsunamis, but the greatest danger comes from collapsing buildings. Scientists record approximately 200,000 earthquakes around the world each year, with hundreds of thousands of smaller quakes going undetected. Nevertheless, a method to predict earthquakes with any significant degree of accuracy has remained **elusive** to scientists.

The forecasting of earthquakes remains a prominent area of interest in geological research. By using information collected from global **seismic** monitoring networks, geological field work, and historical records, seismologists are able to make reasonably accurate forecasts for upcoming years and decades about earthquakes. However, they still lack methods to forecast earthquakes a few days or months in advance accurately. For instance, earthquake models show that the likelihood of Southern California having an earthquake of a 7.5 **magnitude** or greater in the next 30 years is 38 percent. However, the same models state that the odds of such a quake happening within a week are only 0.02 percent.

This uncertainty in short-term forecasting makes it nearly impossible to generate accurate predictions about earthquakes right before they happen. To provide warnings far enough in advance—at least a few minutes—scientists would need to identify **diagnostic precursors**. Thus far, scientists have measured certain changes that occur before earthquakes. These include abnormal animal behavior, such as snakes and mice coming out of their holes, and the release of radon gas, which is produced by uranium. The water in ponds and wells will also bubble prior to earthquakes. However, these factors cannot be used to predict quakes as they also occur without being followed by seismic events. Making more accurate predictions would require scientists to install measurement devices several kilometers below ground. There, they could detect the **shifts** in the Earth's **crust** that cause quakes. This would not only be very difficult to implement but also prohibitively expensive.

While we still cannot predict earthquakes, there are some systems put in place to help people stay safer when one does strike. For example, California has an earthquake early warning (EEW) system to give residents from a few seconds to a few minutes warning before a quake. It uses a system of sensors, and after detecting seismic waves, it sends warnings to people's phones of an impending quake. Perhaps more important is strengthening buildings to withstand earthquakes. Governments must enact regulations requiring new buildings be built strong enough to withstand earthquakes of certain magnitudes. **Words 409**

Reading Skill

*The **main idea** is usually at the beginning of a text and makes a general statement. The **supporting details** are specific ideas that support the main idea.*

Q What are two methods that can keep people safe from earthquakes?
A They are an earthquake early _____ system and the strengthening of buildings to _____ earthquakes.

Vocabulary in Context

A Match the words in bold from the passage with their correct definitions.

1. _____ a change or alteration

2. _____ difficult to find or discover

3. _____ of or relating to an earthquake

4. _____ the moving or shaking of the ground

5. _____ related to identifying a problem

6. _____ the outer or topmost layer of the Earth

7. _____ a measurement of the power or intensity of an earthquake

8. _____ an event that shows another event is going to happen

B Look at the underlined words or phrases in the passage and choose the correct answers.

1. The word underdetected in the first paragraph is closest in meaning to _____.
   a. unfamiliar   b. remarkable   c. mistreated   d. unnoticed

2. The phrase in advance in the second paragraph is closest in meaning to _____.
   a. afterward   b. beforehand   c. virtually   d. specifically

3. The word prohibitively in the third paragraph is closest in meaning to _____.
   a. moderately   b. excessively   c. completely   d. promptly

4. The word impending in the fourth paragraph is closest in meaning to _____.
   a. expected   b. crucial   c. approaching   d. urgent

C Choose the best word to complete each sentence.

1. My parents instilled / installed a sense of good manners and hard work in me as a child.

2. The school will implement / complement a new system to distribute homework to students.

3. Although geological / seismic activity occurs nearly all the time, it rarely results in earthquakes.

Reading Comprehension

Main Idea

1. What is the main idea of the passage?

   a. Earthquakes are deadlier than other type of natural disaster.
   b. Scientists have not yet found a way to anticipate earthquakes accurately.
   c. Global seismic networks offer the most accurate information about future earthquakes.
   d. Research must focus on how to prevent buildings from collapsing during earthquakes.

Details

2. What types of information do seismologists use to make earthquake predictions?

   _____

3. Why does the passage mention the odds of an earthquake happening in California?

   a. to indicate that earthquakes happen frequently in California
   b. to show how earthquake prediction methods have improved greatly in recent years
   c. to highlight that current earthquake predictions are not relevant in the short term
   d. to argue that scientists should use different sources of information to predict earthquakes

4. What does the word **these** in the third paragraph refer to?

   a. warnings   b. earthquakes   c. changes   d. accurate predictions

5. Why can scientists NOT use the changes observed before earthquakes as diagnostic precursors?

   _____

6. Which of the following is true according to the passage?

   a. Scientists can detect and record small earthquakes.
   b. Governments will make older buildings strong enough to withstand earthquakes.
   c. People are more likely to be safe if they are warned a few seconds before an earthquake.
   d. The measurement devices for earthquake early warning systems are installed several kilometers below ground.

Inference

7. What can be inferred from the passage?

   a. Most buildings in many countries can withstand an earthquake.
   b. Scientists have yet to find reliable diagnostic precursors for earthquakes.
   c. The chances of an earthquake happening in the short term is generally unlikely.
   d. Many countries have enough warning systems to keep their people safe from earthquakes.

Summary

A Fill in the chart with the phrases in the box.

	The Difficulty of Predicting Earthquakes
Predicting Earthquakes	• Seismologists can make moderately accurate predictions about earthquakes ❶_____ in advance by looking at geological records. • However, it is still not possible to predict earthquakes ❷_____ or months ahead of time.
Giving Warning	Changes such as ❸_____ have been observed before earthquakes, but scientists would need to install ❹_____ several kilometers below ground to make more accurate predictions.
Systems to Keep People Safe	• Systems such as an earthquake early warning (EEW) system give residents a warning before an earthquake so that they may ❺_____. • Government regulations requiring buildings to be able to ❻_____ will also help people survive.

stay safer   measurement devices   years and decades
a few days   withstand earthquakes   abnormal animal behavior

B Complete the summary with correct words by referring to the chart above.

Earthquakes are the deadliest type of natural disaster, but scientists still cannot ❶_____ them accurately. Seismologists are able to make moderately accurate predictions of earthquakes years and decades in ❷_____. However, they still lack the methods to predict earthquakes a few ❸_____ or months ahead of time. Because of this, it is impossible to predict quakes right before they happen. Scientists have observed certain ❹_____ that occur before quakes, such as unusual animal behavior. However, to make more accurate predictions, they would have to ❺_____ measurement devices several kilometers below ❻_____. Although we cannot predict earthquakes, systems such as an earthquake early warning (EEW) system give residents a ❼_____ before a quake while new building ❽_____ will help structures withstand earthquakes.

Unit 14

Theme | *Linguistics*
Reading Skill | *Compare & Contrast*

Writing Styles Around the World

Before You Read

A Think about the Topic

1. What languages do you know? Is there a difference when you write in them?
2. How does Korean essay writing differ from American essay writing?

B Background Knowledge

Indo-European languages are a group of hundreds of languages spoken by nearly half the world's population. These languages are spoken throughout the Americas, Europe, and parts of Asia. Two of the largest branches of Indo-European languages include Romance languages, which include Spanish, Portuguese, French, and Italian, and Germanic languages, consisting of English, German, and Dutch. The writing styles of these languages have been influenced by ancient Greek philosophers, especially Aristotle's concept of logical reasoning. While this system of writing is prevalent in Western countries, speakers of languages in other parts of the world have developed different approaches to essay writing.

Unit 14
Linguistics | Compare & Contrast

Writing Styles Around the World

▶ *While you read, pay attention to how the writing styles of each language are different.*

In the mid-1900s applied linguist Robert Kaplan developed the **premise** that language and writing are linked to culture. As a result, different cultures have different language styles. Furthermore, he argued that these patterns are carried over when a person uses another language, resulting in errors. Kaplan used this concept to identify different
5 writing styles in languages and then to group them into categories.

Western languages tend to have a more **linear** writing style. Even compared to other Indo-European languages, English writing is very rigid with formalized rules governing the order and layout of compositions. The essay is grouped around a main **thesis**, which is generally stated
10 near the start. This is referred to as deductive writing. In contrast, there are some European languages that place the thesis towards the end, which is called inductive writing. Following this pattern, English writing focuses on the use of discrete paragraphs with each
15 containing a single idea. Stylistically, students are taught that the use of **subordination** is more sophisticated. Using short, **choppy** sentences reflects less development. Students are also

warned against the use of digressions, sentences which do not directly support the main idea. However, both French and German formal writing is filled with digressions. Natives of those countries feel they improve the text. From this, it can be seen that even within related languages, there exists significant diversity.

Not surprisingly, East Asian writing is <u>markedly</u> different from that of English. Most notably, rather than being linear, it is a spiral that eventually **hones in on** the topic. Asian essays often begin with more general information that is only **peripherally** related to the main idea. As the composition develops, the writer continually tightens the focus until reaching the main idea. In addition, Asian writers frequently include **concessions** that raise possible weaknesses in their own arguments. These are not viewed as flaws as they would be in Western-style writing. Instead, ==they== are seen as a reflection of the writer <u>exploring</u> the work in depth.

The most important application of this kind of analysis is to help students who are learning a second language. Teachers who are familiar with the different styles can help identify possible sources of errors in student-generated work. Yet, at the same time, it is important for the teacher not to assume that one writing style is superior to another. **Words 388**

Reading Skill

Comparing and contrasting is a way to explain how two or more things are similar and different.

Q   What is the difference between deductive and inductive writing in essays?
A   Deductive writing requires students to place the thesis near the _____ of the essay whereas inductive writing places the thesis towards the _____.

Unit 14 89

Vocabulary in Context

A **Match the words or phrases in bold from the passage with their correct definitions.**

1. _____ to focus more on over time

2. _____ not flowing smoothly; disconnected

3. _____ an admission of a mistake or flaw

4. _____ not as the main or important part of something

5. _____ going from one thing to another in a direct way

6. _____ the sentence in an essay that expresses the main idea

7. _____ a part of a sentence that acts as a noun, adjective, or adverb

8. _____ a basic theory or idea about what something is or how it works

B **Look at the underlined words in the passage and choose the correct answers.**

1. The word rigid in the second paragraph is closest in meaning to _____.
   a. strict   b. flexible   c. stubborn   d. harsh

2. The word discrete in the second paragraph is closest in meaning to _____.
   a. special   b. partial   c. separate   d. new

3. The word markedly in the third paragraph is closest in meaning to _____.
   a. subtly   b. impressively   c. noticeably   d. considerately

4. The word explore in the third paragraph is closest in meaning to _____.
   a. discover   b. indicate   c. inspect   d. investigate

C **Choose the best word to complete each sentence.**

1. I am continually / regularly worried about finding a good job after graduation.

2. We cannot begin the project until the plans are formalized / finalized by the committee.

3. In English, students are taught that digression / concession weakens the focus of their arguments.

Reading Comprehension

Main Idea

1. **What is the passage mainly about?**

   a. common problems students face with essay writing
   b. the strengths and weaknesses of various composition styles
   c. the superiority of English writing rules compared to other styles
   d. cultural influences on the writing styles of different languages

Details

2. **Which of the following is NOT true about English writing?**

   a. Digression is regarded as a weakness.
   b. It is considered better to use many short sentences.
   c. It has fixed procedures for outlining compositions.
   d. The use of subordination is thought of as more sophisticated.

3. **Why do French and German writers use digressions?**

   _____

4. **What does the word they in the third paragraph refer to?**

   a. concessions   b. Asian writers   c. arguments   d. flaws

5. **Which of the following is NOT true according to the passage?**

   a. East Asian writers intentionally include concessions in their essays.
   b. English and German have developed similar rules for essay composition.
   c. East Asian essays focus on the main idea at the end of the composition.
   d. One writing style should not be considered logically superior to other types.

6. **Why do Asian writers include concessions in their essays?**

   _____

Inference

7. **According to Kaplan, people writing in a foreign language _____.**

   a. make a number of grammar and spelling errors
   b. have difficulty expressing their ideas and emotions
   c. cannot properly identify the correct writing style to use
   d. may unconsciously use the style of their native language

Summary

A **Fill in the chart with the phrases in the box.**

Western Writing vs. Asian Writing

Western Writing
- Western writing generally has a more ❶_____.
- English has formalized ❷_____, with essays grouped around a main thesis.
- English essays have ❸_____, each with its own main idea.
- French and German essays ❹_____ that are not put in English essays.

Asian Writing
- Asian essays use ❺_____, starting with general ideas and gradually focusing on the main idea.
- Writers will include ❻_____ in their own arguments to explore the work in depth.

| possible flaws | linear writing style | distinct paragraphs |
| rules of composition | include digressions | a spiral organization |

B **Complete the summary with correct words by referring to the chart above.**

Applied linguist Robert Kaplan developed the premise that different languages have different writing styles. In general, English and other Indo-European languages have ❶_____ writing styles. English essays have ideas grouped around a ❷_____ that appears near the beginning of the essay, followed by distinct paragraphs. However, some European languages place the thesis near the ❸_____. In terms of style, English writers are expected to use ❹_____ and to avoid ❺_____. On the contrary, East Asian writing has a different style, with writers using a ❻_____ organization. They will start with ❼_____ information relating to the topic, gradually focusing until reaching the ❽_____. Understanding these differences can help students learning foreign languages improve their writing.

Unit 15

Theme | *Technology*
Reading Skill | *Sequencing*

3D Printed Organs

Before You Read

A Think about the Topic

1. What are some of the benefits of 3D printing technology?
2. How do you think 3D printing technology can be used in the field of medicine?

B Background Knowledge

The science of medicine has always been advanced by the development of technology. From the invention of the first microscopes and surgical techniques to the discovery of vaccines, medical advancements have helped save the lives of millions of people. One remaining problem is replacing injured organs. There are currently two main methods. One is getting replacement organs from other people and implanting them into the body. The other is using artificial organs to take the place of certain body parts. However, these methods are expensive and have a high rate of failure. To make replacing organs easier and more likely to succeed, scientists have been developing methods to produce organs by using 3D printing technology.

Unit 15
Technology | Sequencing

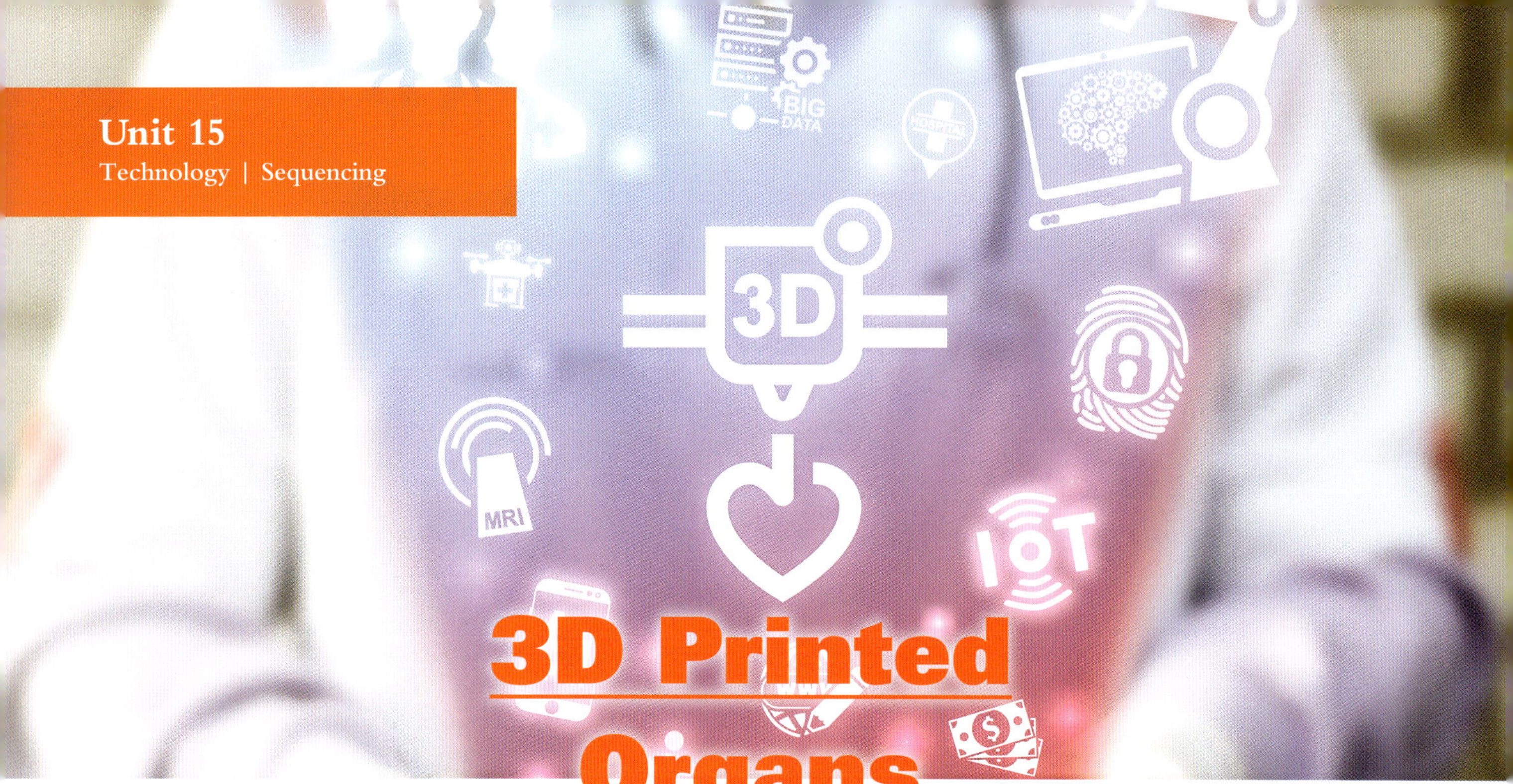

3D Printed Organs

▶ *While you read, focus on how 3D organs are produced and what applications they have for our health.*

Across the world, thousands of people are waiting for organ **transplants**. Those who do receive a replacement organ in time might still run into problems with their bodies rejecting the organ. To **rectify** this situation and save lives, scientists have begun researching methods of applying 3D technology to print organs for transplant. Although the technology is still in its infancy, scientists have found several applications for it that can increase people's chances for survival.

Most 3D organ printing technology is based on existing 3D printing techniques with some key differences. Instead of using plastic compounds as in other types of 3D printing, researchers use water-based gels containing live cells as ink in 3D printers to layer **them**

in a specific pattern. Over time, the gels break down, and the natural cells expand, growing into full organs. This happens since cells will naturally **fuse** together when placed in the appropriate pattern and grow into **tissue** and organs that the body can use. For instance, if you arrange enough ear cells in roughly the correct shape, they will eventually grow into an ear. By allowing nutrients and oxygen to flow through these organs, they can be integrated into the bodies of humans and animals.

To date, 3D printing technology has been used to recreate the structures of organs on a single-cell level. Scientists have also been able to produce cells that divide to create a **cell culture**. The easiest organ to print is human skin, which has been transplanted onto the burns of humans. In another case, one researcher successfully printed and transplanted living bone tissue into artificial jaws. This has been used to rebuild the jawbones of patients who need dental **implants**.

Creating more complex internal organs, such as whole hearts, livers, and **kidneys**, has proven too difficult with current technology. However, scientists have managed to print parts of these organs which could soon be used to repair patients' organs. For example, they have used stem cells from the liver to emulate the functions of the liver. Scientists currently speculate that the first functioning 3D-printed internal organ could occur within the next decade. The organ most likely to be printed successfully is the *bladder as it is relatively simple compared to other organs.

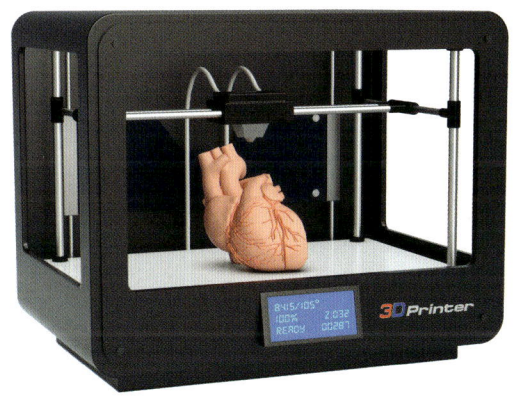

The future looks bright for 3D organ technology. Someday, it will be used to save people's lives after they **develop** cancer or get into accidents. It may also be used to enhance our natural organs so that we may become stronger and live longer. **Words 416**

*bladder: the organ that holds urine after it goes through the kidneys

Reading Skill

Sequencing is putting events in order from first to last. When we sequence, we can easily understand which events happen first, second, and so on.

Q What happens after 3D printers arrange water-based gels in a specific pattern?
A The gels will break down eventually and the _____ will expand and grow into tissue and _____.

Vocabulary in Context

A Match the words or phrases in bold from the passage with their correct definitions.

1. _____ to grow together or join

2. _____ the material that makes up a living creature

3. _____ something added to the body through surgery

4. _____ to start to have something such as a disease

5. _____ a group of cells growing in an artificial environment

6. _____ to make a wrong situation become right; to correct

7. _____ the organ that removes waste products to clean the blood

8. _____ an operation in which an internal organ of someone is replaced with one from another person

B Look at the underlined words in the passage and choose the correct answers.

1. The word infancy in the first paragraph is closest in meaning to _____.
   a. final steps   b. popularity   c. early stages   d. revolution

2. The word integrate in the second paragraph is closest in meaning to _____.
   a. join   b. enhance   c. exist   d. reject

3. The word emulate in the fourth paragraph is closest in meaning to _____.
   a. reflect   b. imitate   c. access   d. expect

4. The word speculate in the fourth paragraph is closest in meaning to _____.
   a. wonder   b. risk   c. predict   d. assure

C Choose the best word or phrase to complete each sentence.

1. Once you complete your arranged / assigned task, you can go home for the day.

2. Toddlers can run into / run out problems if they drink a lot of milk and only eat a little meat.

3. The doctors successfully transplanted / transformed the kidney during an operation that lasted for four hours.

Reading Comprehension

Main Idea

1. What is the passage mainly about?

   a. the problems of relying on organ transplants for patients
   b. how a new technology is making medical procedures easier
   c. new applications for 3D printing technology in various fields
   d. ways to increase the chances of a person's body accepting an organ

Details

2. According to the passage, which is NOT true about using 3D printers to make organs?

   a. Any 3D printer can be used to make printed organs.
   b. Printing organs requires the use of water-based gels.
   c. The cells in the printing gels will join naturally over time.
   d. Scientists have been able to recreate organ structures on a single-cell level.

3. Why is it important to allow nutrients and oxygen to pass through organs?

   _____

4. What does the word **them** in the second paragraph refer to?

   a. organs   b. compounds   c. live cells   d. water-based gels

5. How has 3D printing been used so far to treat patients?

   _____

6. In paragraph 4, the author states that _____.

   a. 3D printed organs will impair patients' organ functions
   b. scientists have been able to print a functioning bladder successfully
   c. it will soon be possible to print hearts, livers, and other internal organs
   d. using stem cells makes it possible to reproduce the functions of organs

Inference

7. What can be inferred from the passage?

   a. Printing gels are used to enhance the strength of printed organs.
   b. 3D organ printing technology will probably increase people's lifespans.
   c. 3D organ printing technology is totally different from that of existing 3D printing.
   d. Only people who have serious illnesses will benefit from 3D organ printing technology.

Unit 15   97

Summary

A Fill in the chart with the phrases in the box.

3D Printed Organs	
How It Works	• Scientists use existing 3D technology to layer water-based gels containing ❶_____ in the shape of organs. • These gels eventually break down, and the live cells ❷_____, allowing tissue and organs to grow.
Current Accomplishments	• Currently, scientists have reproduced organ structures on a ❸_____ and have transplanted skin and bone tissue. • For instance, one scientist used bone tissue to ❹_____ of patients.
Future Developments	• With current technology, it is not possible to create more ❺_____, such as livers and kidneys. • However, scientists may soon be able to print parts of organs and to create a ❻_____ in the next decade.

    live cells   functioning bladder   rebuild the jawbones
    fuse together   single-cell level   complex internal organs

B Complete the summary with correct words by referring to the chart above.

Scientists have been researching methods to use 3D printing technology to create ❶_____ for transplants. They use 3D printing techniques to ❷_____ water-based gels containing live cells in a specific pattern. These gels ❸_____ down, and the cells naturally fuse together over time, growing into ❹_____ and organs. So far, scientists have been able to reproduce organ ❺_____ on a single-cell level and have successfully printed ❻_____ and bone tissue. Making more complex ❼_____ organs, such as livers and kidneys, is not possible with current technology. However, scientists may soon be able to print parts of organs to repair patients' organs. It is estimated that scientists will be able to print a functioning ❽_____ in the next decade.

Unit 16

Theme | *Biology*
Reading Skill | *Categorizing*

Ocean Zones and Their Characteristics

Before You Read

A Think about the Topic

1. What do you know about the oceans or ocean life?
2. What are the possible benefits of studying this vast aquatic habitat?

B Background Knowledge

The World Ocean covers roughly 70 percent of Earth's surface. Comprising just seven percent of the area of the World Ocean are coastal oceans. As their name suggests, these are the parts of the oceans closest to land. These areas contain most of the types of environments that people imagine when they think of the oceans. While coastal oceans make up only a small part of the World Ocean, they are home to 90 percent of the oceans' animal life. The biodiversity in the coastal oceans provides food for many types of animals, including humans. As important as the costal oceans are, the rest of the World Ocean still contains a huge variety of marine life.

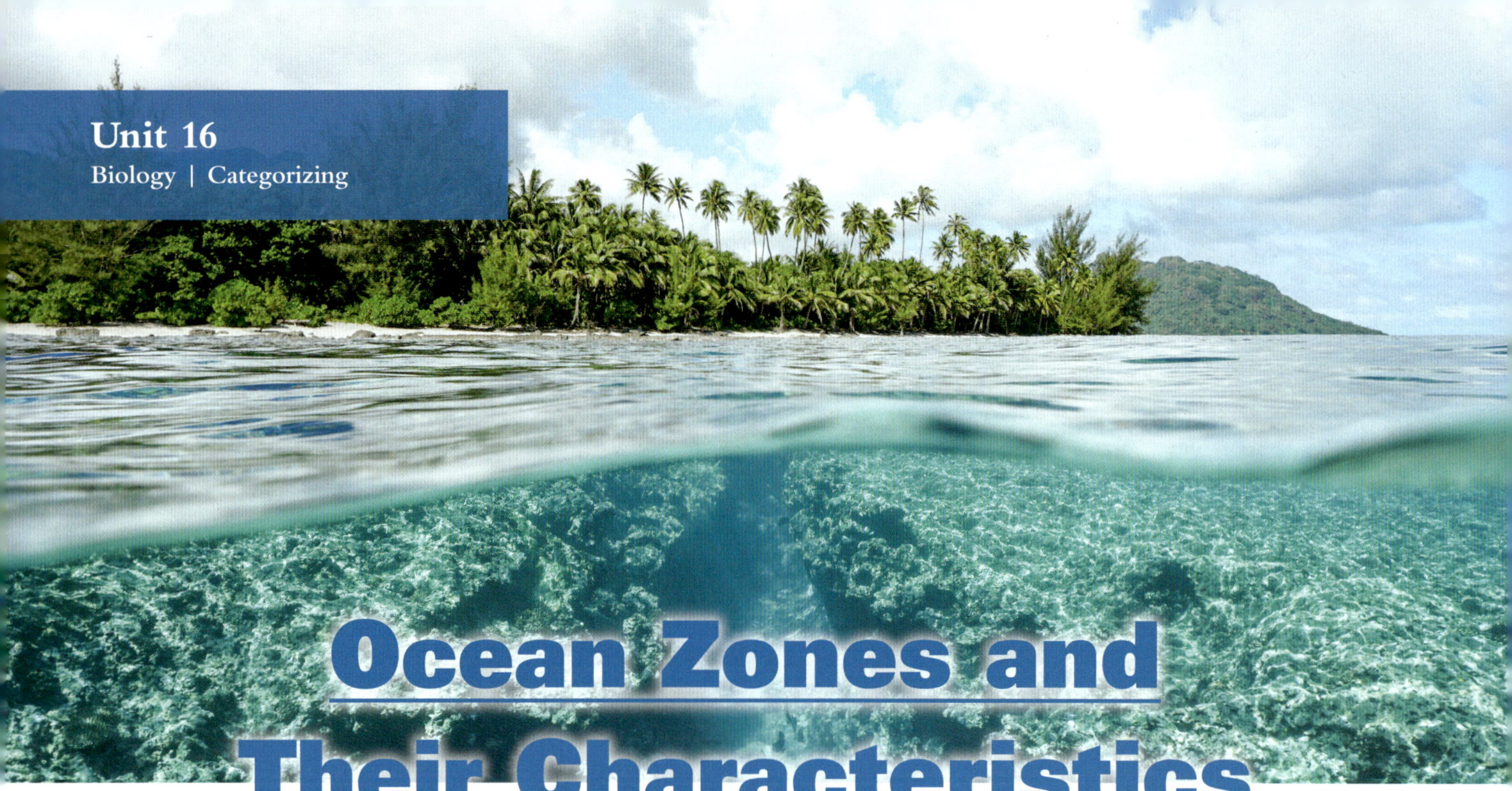

Unit 16
Biology | Categorizing

Ocean Zones and Their Characteristics

▶ *While you read, pay attention to the differences in the environment and animals in the various ocean zones.*

The coastal oceans make up less than one-tenth of the total volume of the World Ocean while the remainder is termed the open ocean. That region lacks the complex life and diversity found along the coasts. Nevertheless, this ecosystem is still unique and home to a wide variety of species.

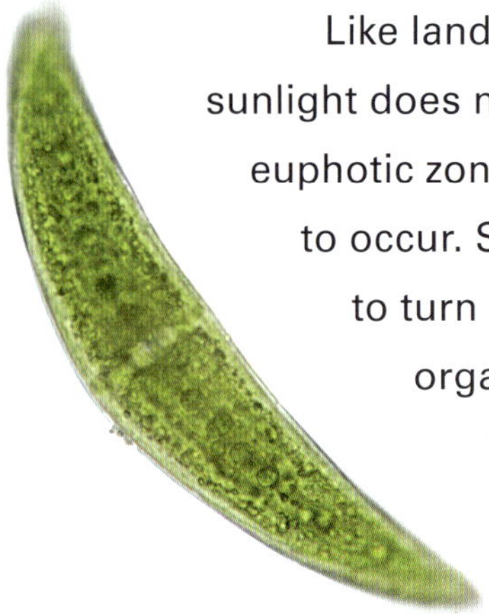

Like land animals, most life in the open ocean relies upon sunlight. However, sunlight does not **penetrate** deeply under the water. Consequently, only the euphotic zone, the upper layer, receives enough sunlight for photosynthesis to occur. Single-celled organisms called phytoplankton use photosynthesis to turn sunlight and carbon dioxide into energy and oxygen. These tiny organisms form the basis of the food chain. Because of the wealth of food, over 90 percent of all open ocean life lives in this layer. In addition, the warm waters and low pressure enable a wide range of life to survive in comparison to other parts of the ocean, which are less **hospitable**.

▲ phytoplankton

Starting from approximately 200 meters down to 1,000 meters is the disphotic zone. As only minimal light reaches this layer, organisms living there have made several remarkable adaptations. Some species are able to swim up to the euphotic zone to feed,

▲ The cuttlefish living in the disphotic zone

and others have developed bioluminescence, a physical process that generates light. For example, the firefly squid has specialized light-generating cells that it uses to attract prey as well as to **camouflage** itself. Bioluminescent animals also rely on counter-**illumination** to avoid predators. They generate light on the bottom parts of their bodies that matches the brightness of the light from above while keeping their top parts unlit. This makes the animal appear nearly invisible to predators below it.

In the deepest region of the open ocean, the aphotic zone, there are extremely high pressure, near-freezing temperatures, and virtually no light. Since these conditions are so harsh, scientists long believed that few species could survive there. However, improved technology has enabled scientists to dive deep below the open ocean's surface. They have found some species that are able to survive by eating the **detritus** that comes from the upper regions. They have also discovered underground **vents**, which are cracks in the ocean floor that emit high-temperature water and are rich in chemicals. Some bacteria are able to use their *hydrogen sulphide in a process that is similar to photosynthesis. Those bacteria can then serve as the basis of an underwater food chain. As a result, scientists have **located** a few **pockets** of deep-underwater life that display a startling amount of biodiversity.

Words 418

▲ An anglerfish living in the aphotic zone

*hydrogen sulphide: a colorless gas that smells like rotten eggs and is very poisonous and flammable

Reading Skill

Categorizing information means to arrange information or items into different groups.

- **Q** What are the classifications of ocean water based on the amount of sunlight they receive?
- **A** The euphotic zone receives enough sunlight for _____ to occur, the disphotic zone receives minimal light, and the _____ zone receives virtually no light.

Unit 16 **101**

Vocabulary in Context

A **Match the words in bold from the passage with their correct definitions.**

1. _____ to find where something is

2. _____ to go through or into something

3. _____ light that shines into a place, from something, etc.

4. _____ a small area in which something different is located

5. _____ pieces that are left when something breaks, falls apart, etc.

6. _____ an opening through which air, steam, water, etc. can escape

7. _____ to hide something by making it hard to see or by making it look like things around it

8. _____ having an environment that makes it easy for plants and animals to live in

B **Look at the underlined words in the passage and choose the correct answers.**

1. The word volume in the first paragraph is closest in meaning to _____.
   a. content   b. amount   c. liquid   d. density

2. The word remainder in the first paragraph is closest in meaning to _____.
   a. excess   b. depth   c. bulk   d. leftover

3. The word wealth in the second paragraph is closest in meaning to _____.
   a. limit   b. abundance   c. diversity   d. frequency

4. The word startling in the fourth paragraph is closest in meaning to _____.
   a. expected   b. notable   c. astonishing   d. ordinary

C **Choose the best word to complete each sentence.**

1. This new application will help you locate / place your phone if you lose it.

2. The variety / variation of foods available at buffets can be overwhelming sometimes.

3. Due to the virtually / severely cold temperatures, school has been canceled today.

Reading Comprehension

Main Idea

1. **What is the passage mainly about?**

    a. the different ocean zones and how life is supported in each
    b. the characteristics of coastal oceans compared to the open ocean
    c. animals that are able to survive in environments with extreme conditions
    d. how scientific research about the open ocean has improved in recent years

Details

2. **Why does the majority of ocean life reside in the euphotic zone?**

    _____

3. **Which of the following is true according to the passage?**

    a. Over 90 percent of ocean animals need photosynthesis to survive.
    b. The aphotic zone has temperatures that are well above freezing.
    c. Bioluminescence makes it difficult for predators to see animals from above.
    d. Some animals in the deep ocean rely on leftover food from above to survive.

4. **What adaptations have animals in the disphotic zone made to survive?**

    _____

5. **What does the word their in the fourth paragraph refer to?**

    a. chemicals   b. species   c. bacteria   d. vents

6. **According to paragraph 4, underground vents are _____.**

    a. being studied currently to see if they provide clues about other ocean life
    b. largely responsible and necessary for maintaining life in the aphotic zone
    c. important for organisms living in the coastal oceans and in the euphotic zone
    d. one of the primary reasons why scientists now know more about the disphotic zone

Inference

7. **What can be inferred from the passage?**

    a. Deeper oceans have higher temperatures and pressure.
    b. Scientists believed that no species could live in the aphotic zone.
    c. Life is not evenly distributed throughout the deepest parts of the ocean.
    d. Larger animals are better suited to survive in the deeper ocean areas.

Summary

A   Fill in the chart with the phrases in the box.

Ocean Zones and Their Characteristics	
The Open Ocean	It accounts for a majority of Earth's ❶_____ and is rich with life.
Euphotic Zone	A majority of open ocean life lives near the surface owing to the abundance of ❷_____, as well as the warm waters and low pressure.
Disphotic Zone	Only ❸_____ reaches this layer, so animals have ❹_____ such as bioluminescence that help them to survive.
Aphotic Zone	There are high pressure, ❺_____ temperatures, and no light. But life still exists in this area once believed to contain very little sea life thanks to ❻_____.

near-freezing   underground vents   minimal sunlight
sunlight and food   made adaptations   ocean waters

B   Complete the summary with correct words by referring to the chart above.

The ❶_____ ocean is a rich, immense, and layered aquatic habitat. Scientists have split the ocean into three zones which correspond to how much ❷_____ each receives. Most ocean life lives in the uppermost, or euphotic zone, which receives the most sunlight and has the warmest ❸_____. The next zone is the disphotic zone. Since only ❹_____ light reaches this level, animals have developed bioluminescence to attract ❺_____ and to provide camouflage. In the ❻_____ part of the ocean, the aphotic zone, there is almost no light, and temperatures are near freezing. Because of these conditions, scientists long thought that ❼_____ animals lived there. Thanks to recent technological developments, however, scientists discovered pockets of ❽_____ around underground vents.

Developing Background Knowledge and Reading Strategies

Reading

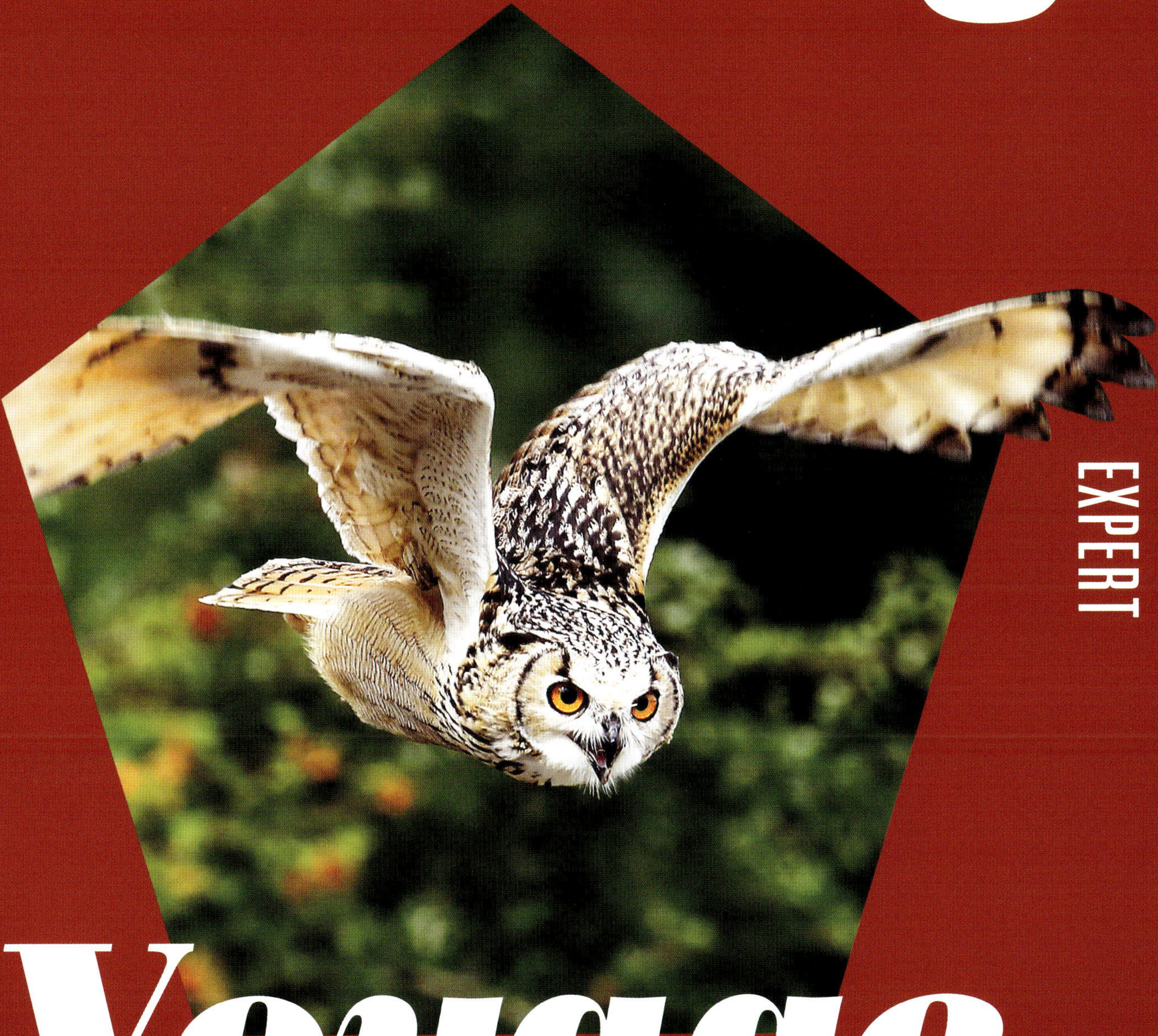

EXPERT

Voyage

2

DARAKWON

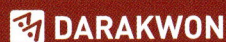

WORKBOOK

Unit 1: Virtual Reality vs. Augmented Reality

Vocabulary Practice

A Write each word next to its correct definition. Then write its meaning in your language.

virtual	coin	overlay	overlap	mounted
prime	gear	immersive	interact	remotely
pioneer	field	augment	manipulate	interchangeably

1. typical; main _____ _____
2. from a distance _____ _____
3. existing on computers _____ _____
4. to control something skillfully _____ _____
5. installed or attached to something _____ _____
6. to create a new term or expression _____ _____
7. to cover one thing with something else _____ _____
8. to have some similarities or things in common _____ _____
9. in a way that can be switched or changed easily _____ _____
10. equipment or accessories for a specific purpose _____ _____
11. be the first to do, invent, or use something _____ _____
12. to make something greater by adding to it; to increase _____ _____
13. making the audience feel completely involved in something _____ _____
14. to act with someone or something else, each affecting the other's next action _____ _____
15. an academic or professional area of interest, such as a doctor in the medical field _____ _____

Writing Practice

B Circle the correct words and translate the sentences into your language.

1. These technologies are changing the way people interact (to / **with**) digital content.
   ➤ _____

2. Although VR and AR technologies (overlay / **overlap**) in some ways, there are several key differences between them.
   ➤ _____

3. A prime example of the (**application** / applicant) of AR technology in our daily lives is the smartphone game *Pokémon GO*.
   ➤ _____

4. (**While** / If) VR technology creates a separate world, AR combines computer graphics and digital images with real environments.
   ➤ _____

More Reading Comprehension

C Read the passage and answer the questions.

> Both VR and AR rely on computer graphics and visual displays, but they utilize those technologies in opposite ways. (A) <u>As</u> the name implies, virtual reality uses computer graphics to create a simulation of real life or imaginary environments. To accomplish this, VR is usually (B) <u>experiencing</u> through a head-mounted display and motion-sensing controls. This method of display (C) <u>provides</u> a more immersive experience and makes users feel as if they are interacting with the environment (D) <u>firsthand</u>. Today, VR is used for _____ purposes, such as gaming and 3D movies. It is also used to provide training for real-life environments, such as flight simulators for pilots.

1. Which is the most appropriate for the blank?

   a. medical   b. research   c. entertainment   d. academic

2. Which one is NOT grammatically correct in the passage?

   a. (A)   b. (B)   c. (C)   d. (D)

Unit 2

Eye Makeup in Ancient Civilizations

Vocabulary Practice

A Write each word or phrase next to its correct definition. Then write its meaning in your language.

covet	curse	afflict	vessel	prominent
gaze at	bestow	glance	uncover	hieroglyphic
element	drastic	ward off	compound	anthropologist

1. an object used as a container _____ _____

2. a scientist who studies humans _____ _____

3. to give someone something _____ _____

4. highly noticeable; well-known _____ _____

5. extreme and sudden in effect or action _____ _____

6. to look at for a long time out of curiosity _____ _____

7. a specific part of a situation or activity _____ _____

8. the act of looking at something for a moment _____ _____

9. to affect someone badly and to make that person suffer _____ _____

10. a writing system that uses pictures instead of words _____ _____

11. to want something that you do not own very much _____ _____

12. magical words that are thought to cause harm or bad luck _____ _____

13. to prevent something negative from happening or occurring; to defend against _____ _____

14. to find or discover something that was hidden for a long time _____ _____

15. a substance made up of many different ingredients or materials _____ _____

Writing Practice

B Circle the correct words and translate the sentences into your language.

1. Roman women used mascara to make their eyelashes more (promising / **prominent**).

    ➢ _____

2. Its chemicals could shield eyes (**from** / for) the harsh sunlight of the Egyptian desert.

    ➢ _____

3. An extreme defense against the evil eye was mothers (spit / **spitting**) in a stranger's face.

    ➢ _____

4. Over time, makeup was worn to enhance beauty by drawing attention (**to** / at) certain facial features.

    ➢ _____

More Reading Comprehension

C Read the passage and answer the questions.

> In ancient Greece, men and women from higher social classes would wear eye shadow for decorative purposes. They would apply ground charcoal mixed with olive oil and different colored herbs as eye shadow. _____ the Greeks did not wear eye shadow for protection, they still believed that exaggerated eye shapes could ward off evil. For instance, archaeologists have uncovered sixth-century black-figured drinking vessels decorated with eyes. **They** believe the drawings were meant to prevent evil spirits from entering the drinker's body, protecting the drinker from consuming poison.

1. Which is the most appropriate for the blank?

    a. When   b. Since   c. If   d. Although

2. What does the word **They** refer to?

    a. archaeologists   b. vessels   c. the Greeks   d. eye shapes

Unit 3: The Continuing Problem of Slavery

Vocabulary Practice

A Write each word or phrase next to its correct definition. Then write its meaning in your language.

lax	will	persist	assemble	clamp down on
enslave	outlaw	bonded	grassroots	labor-intensive
sanction	quarrying	trafficking	predominant	enforcement

1. most noticeable; prime _____ _____
2. desire or agreement _____ _____
3. to gather people _____ _____
4. to make someone a slave _____ _____
5. to continue to exist _____ _____
6. not strict or careful about rules _____ _____
7. needing a lot of work or workers _____ _____
8. to officially permit or approve _____ _____
9. to make something against the law; to prohibit _____ _____
10. obligated by a debt to serve without wages _____ _____
11. the act of buying and selling something illegally _____ _____
12. the act of making sure that people follow rules or laws _____ _____
13. the business or activity of digging stones out of the ground _____ _____
14. to take action to stop an activity or the people doing an activity _____ _____
15. the lowest level of organization, usually involving common people _____ _____

Writing Practice

B Circle the correct words and translate the sentences into your language.

1. There is hope for the millions of people (enslaved / enslaving) around the world.

    ➤ _____

2. Slavery (sustains / persists) in these countries due to the lax enforcement of anti-slavery laws.

    ➤ _____

3. The number of slaves globally (is / are) estimated to be between 21 and 46 million people.

    ➤ _____

4. You can donate your time and money to these organizations to (vanish / banish) slavery from our world once and for all.

    ➤ _____

More Reading Comprehension

C Read the passage and answer the questions.

> Just as slavery exists in many places, there are many reasons that people are enslaved. Perhaps the most widespread type of slavery is forced labor. This is when people are (A) <u>forcing</u> to do work, often with no payment, (B) <u>against</u> their will under the threat of some form of punishment. ⓐ It most frequently occurs in labor-intensive and under-regulated industries, including agriculture and fishing; domestic work; construction, mining, quarrying, and brick kilns; and manufacturing. ⓑ Perhaps the oldest form of slavery is bonded labor. ⓒ Even though the value of their labor often (C) <u>exceeds</u> the amount of their debt, bonded laborers work for little or no pay. ⓓ In many cases, the debts are passed (D) <u>onto</u> the following generations, meaning that the children of bonded laborers must become bonded laborers themselves.

1. Which is the best place for the sentence?

    > *This is when people are asked to work to repay a debt.*

    a. ⓐ   b. ⓑ   c. ⓒ   d. ⓓ

2. Which one is NOT grammatically correct in the passage?

    a. (A)   b. (B)   c. (C)   d. (D)

Unit 3 7

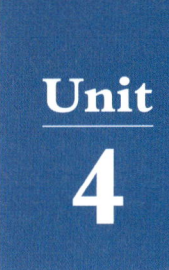

Unit 4 Urbanization and Its Results

Vocabulary Practice

A Write each word or phrase next to its correct definition. Then write its meaning in your language.

array	influx	undertaking	untold	real estate
resident	foremost	transformation	accompany	accommodate
well-off	tenement	demographic	enterprise	out of the market

1. land or buildings _____ _____
2. a massive change _____ _____
3. main or most important _____ _____
4. too many to count; uncountable _____ _____
5. a person living in a place _____ _____
6. related to population patterns _____ _____
7. having plenty of money; wealthy _____ _____
8. a business or similar organization _____ _____
9. a large group or variety of things _____ _____
10. to provide room for someone to stay _____ _____
11. an important or challenging job or task _____ _____
12. the arrival of a large number of people or things _____ _____
13. a large building divided into apartments for the urban poor _____ _____
14. to happen or appear at the same time as something _____ _____
15. to make a price too high for certain groups of people to afford   price someone _____ _____

8

Writing Practice

B Circle the correct words and translate the sentences into your language.

1. No realistic road construction plan could meet the demand (of / **for**) transportation.
   ➤ _____

2. Untold thousands of new businesses started, bringing (in / **about**) an economic boom.
   ➤ _____

3. Decisions (**made** / making) in the City have had a great effect on the global economy.
   ➤ _____

4. There was massive construction of housing to (accompany / **accommodate**) the newcomers.
   ➤ _____

More Reading Comprehension

C Read the passage and answer the questions.

> The new urban growth created a city sharply divided by _____. The number of wealthy people grew from the fabulous profits of the new businesses and land rents. ⓐ The middle class also expanded because the economy needed technical specialists, managers, lawyers, and other professionals. ⓑ Businesses required a great deal of new office and storage space. ⓒ These developments made it impossible for the city's poor and working class majority to live in the central areas, so most residents had to move out of the city center into areas informally designated for the less well-off. ⓓ

1. Which is the most appropriate for the blank?

   a. social class   b. race   c. jobs   d. education

2. Which is the best place for the sentence?

   > *These factors caused rents to rise dramatically, and many houses in central London were worth millions of dollars in today's prices.*

   a. ⓐ   b. ⓑ   c. ⓒ   d. ⓓ

Unit 5: Why Businesses Offer Free Samples

Vocabulary Practice

A Write each word or phrase next to its correct definition. Then write its meaning in your language.

boost	logic	associate	top dollar	hand out
freebie	compel	awareness	reciprocate	presumably
obliged	initially	hold on to	generosity	complimentary

1. given for free
2. from the start; at first
3. probably or apparently
4. to increase; to enhance
5. a very high price
6. to continue believing something
7. something given away at no cost
8. the state of knowing about something
9. feeling that you must do something
10. to give out or distribute something
11. the act of treating someone well; kindness
12. to think of one thing along with something else
13. the correct or proper way to think about something
14. to cause people to do something; to motivate them
15. to do something for someone who has done something for you

Writing Practice

B Circle the correct words or phrases and translate the sentences into your language.

1. Companies that give (away / in) freebies will actually have higher sales.

   ➤ _____

2. Free samples are effective since they compel people (buying / to buy) more.

   ➤ _____

3. People are willing to pay a high price for a product later (if / even though) they get it free initially.

   ➤ _____

4. Whenever people receive something free, they feel (obliging / obliged) to reciprocate the generosity of this act.

   ➤ _____

More Reading Comprehension

C Read the passage and answer the questions.

> The final benefit of freebies is the increase in word-of-mouth marketing. Due to the rise of social media, companies have realized the power of having customers spread the word about their products online. People sometimes use social networking sites to share their experiences using certain products with their friends, thereby increasing _____ of those brands. Companies have found that the most effective way of getting customers to talk about their products with their friends is to give **them** away. For instance, one article in the *Journal of Marketing* found that those who got a product for free were 20 percent more likely to talk about it, and those who got a freebie tied to the product talked about it 15 percent more often.

1. Which is the most appropriate for the blank?

   a. association   b. awareness   c. purchase   d. quality

2. What does the word **them** refer to?

   a. customers   b. friends   c. companies   d. products

Unit 5 11

Unit 6: The Chinese Terracotta Warriors

Vocabulary Practice

A Write each word or phrase next to its correct definition. Then write its meaning in your language.

iris	pupil	edifice	hollow	adhesive
lifelike	armor	generic	stylize	mausoleum
fashion	torso	replicate	abundance	stand guard

1. a large building or structure _____ _____
2. looking similar to a living creature _____ _____
3. to make something using one's hands _____ _____
4. the colored, round part of the eye _____ _____
5. relating to a whole group of things; common _____ _____
6. empty on the inside; having only an outside _____ _____
7. the black, round area in the center of the eye _____ _____
8. to stand in a position to watch and protect someone or something _____ _____
9. being sticky and able to hold other things together _____ _____
10. to remake or reproduce something with great accuracy _____ _____
11. a building in which the bodies of dead people are buried _____ _____
12. a piece of clothing made from metal to protect against attacks _____ _____
13. the main part of the human body without the head, arms, or legs _____ _____
14. the state of being larger or more than needed in size, amount, etc. _____ _____
15. to make something look like a pattern or type rather than appear natural _____ _____

Writing Practice

B Circle the correct words and translate the sentences into your language.

1. It is the soldiers (that / what) continue to awe visitors who come to see them.

   ➤ _____

2. Each soldier was given actual weapons made of bronze, which (was / were) quite advanced for the period.

   ➤ _____

3. The heat had to be carefully controlled (since / although) higher temperatures would have caused the clay to become uneven.

   ➤ _____

4. Despite understanding the (possess / processes), researchers are still unable to replicate these stunning figures.

   ➤ _____

More Reading Comprehension

C Read the passage and answer the questions.

> The construction of the warriors mostly took place in northern China near the site of the tomb. The area had an abundance of clay and loess, which is extremely flexible and adhesive and is ideal for the creation of statues.
> (1) Once partially dry, strips of clay were (A) <u>wound</u> upward to create a hollow body with the exterior smoothed out using flat paddles. Then, various tools were used to create the appearance of armor on the flattened surface.
> (2) Work on the figures proceeded in a series of stages. The feet were fashioned first on a square base with the legs (B) <u>added</u> afterward.
> (3) Next, the heads and hands were pasted on the torso. While each head was generic, it underwent a complicated procedure to make (C) <u>it</u> unique. Each of the 8,000 warriors (D) <u>have</u> a different face.

1. Which one is the correct order for the passage?

   a. (1) – (2) – (3)   b. (1) – (3) – (2)   c. (2) – (1) – (3)   d. (2) – (3) – (1)

2. Which one is NOT grammatically correct in the passage?

   a. (A)   b. (B)   c. (C)   d. (D)

Unit 7: Terrorism, the New World War

Vocabulary Practice

A Write each word next to its correct definition. Then write its meaning in your language.

justify	instill	absent	alienated	respectively
hijack	warrant	detain	ideological	fragmented
fulfill	altruism	initiate	indiscriminate	self-righteous

1. not present; not existing _____ _____
2. to start or begin a process _____ _____
3. to give reasons to explain something _____ _____
4. broken into many pieces or groups _____ _____
5. to take control of or steal a moving vehicle _____ _____
6. to do something required or necessary _____ _____
7. to gradually cause someone to have a feeling or attitude _____ _____
8. in the same order as the people or things mentioned _____ _____
9. to keep someone in a place, usually for questioning by the police _____ _____
10. a desire to help others without the hope of personal benefit _____ _____
11. relating to a set of beliefs or ideas based on political attitude _____ _____
12. affecting or harming many people without care or consideration _____ _____
13. a document given by a court to give the police power to do something _____ _____
14. referring to a person who feels he or she does not belong in a society _____ _____
15. having a strong belief that your opinions are right and others are wrong _____ _____

Writing Practice

B Circle the correct words and translate the sentences into your language.

1. Terrorists often attack visible targets that symbolize (that / **what**) they oppose.

   ➤ _____

2. Another 9,700 and 7,600 such incidents occurred in Pakistan and Afghanistan (**respectively** / respectably).

   ➤ _____

3. Having a sense of self-righteous sacrifice (allow / **allows**) them to justify the violence they commit.

   ➤ _____

4. Terrorism is the use of indiscriminate violence by non-government groups to instill fear (to / **into**) the public to fulfill political goals.

   ➤ _____

More Reading Comprehension

C Read the passage and answer the questions.

> The United States and other nations have (A) <u>initiated</u> a "war on terror" in response to these threats. Also referred to as counter-terrorism measures, anti-terrorism laws have given hundreds of government organizations the means to collect information and to (B) <u>detained</u> suspected terrorists without having warrants. The number of terrorist attacks has somewhat decreased since the initiation of the war on terror. _____, critics contend that most terrorist groups are too fragmented and attacks too unpredictable (C) <u>to defend</u> against fully. Because of this, many feel that anti-terrorism laws have simply given the government too much power to (D) <u>spy on</u> ordinary citizens.

1. Which is the most appropriate for the blank?

   a. Nevertheless   b. Thus   c. In addition   d. In the end

2. Which one is NOT grammatically correct in the passage?

   a. (A)   b. (B)   c. (C)   d. (D)

Unit 8

What IQ and EQ Tests Actually Determine

Vocabulary Practice

A Write each word next to its correct definition. Then write its meaning in your language.

spawn	allot	invalid	assume	methodology
skew	render	constitute	quotient	administer
consensus	bias	rationale	hypothetical	prevalence

1. reasons for something _____ _____
2. not real but imaginary _____ _____
3. to create another similar thing _____ _____
4. to manage or organize something; to execute _____ _____
5. to make something favor one group or result _____ _____
6. not correct or proper due to a flaw or error _____ _____
7. the state of being widely accepted or popular _____ _____
8. to make up something; to comprise something _____ _____
9. to give out something for others to use or have _____ _____
10. the degree of a characteristic in someone or something _____ _____
11. to believe something to be true without direct proof _____ _____
12. to cause something to be in a particular condition or state _____ _____
13. an idea that all the people in a group agree with; agreement _____ _____
14. the process or method by which something such as a test is done _____ _____
15. the tendency to believe that certain groups are better than others and should be treated differently _____ _____

Writing Practice

B Circle the correct words and translate the sentences into your language.

1. Points are (allotting / **allotted**) to how emotionally appropriate the given response is.

   ➤ _____

2. (**Despite** / Due to) the prevalence of these tests, many psychologists still debate the rationale behind IQ and EQ testing.

   ➤ _____

3. Intelligence testing is based on the belief (**that** / when) a person's intelligence can be calculated.

   ➤ _____

4. (Opponents / **Proponents**) of IQ testing argue that the results are accurate predictors of a person's academic ability.

   ➤ _____

More Reading Comprehension

C Read the passage and answer the questions.

> Critics of these tests argue that both tests have serious flaws that render **them** useless. Considering that there is no consensus as to what constitutes intelligence, they claim all the tests are invalid. ⓐThey also point to the fact that people's scores on the same subjects vary from test to test. ⓑOpponents also cite the biases in the tests as IQ test scores are skewed to favor those from specific social and cultural backgrounds. ⓒAs a result, some researchers propose adding classes to improve students' EQ. ⓓEQ tests can be "faked good," a term used to describe how test takers lie to raise their scores.

1. Which sentence is NOT needed in the passage?

   a. ⓐ   b. ⓑ   c. ⓒ   d. ⓓ

2. What does the word **them** refer to?

   a. critics   b. tests   c. flaws   d. scores

Unit 9: The Different Forms of Satire

Vocabulary Practice

A Write each word or phrase next to its correct definition. Then write its meaning in your language.

skit	folly	literary	peculiar	gender equality
wit	dispute	hypocrisy	distinguish	inconsequential
mock	sarcasm	contemporary	institution	hold someone up to ridicule

1. strange or unusual _____ _____
2. relating to literature _____ _____
3. foolish or illogical behavior _____ _____
4. a short comedic performance _____ _____
5. an argument or disagreement _____ _____
6. happening in recent times; modern _____ _____
7. not very important or significant _____ _____
8. to show how one thing is different from another _____ _____
9. the intelligent use of language for humorous effect _____ _____
10. to criticize someone in a humorous but mean way _____ _____
11. the idea that men and women should be treated equally _____ _____
12. to make fun of someone or something to point out their flaws _____ _____
13. behavior that does not match with what someone claims to believe _____ _____
14. the use of words that are the opposite of what you mean to insult someone _____ _____
15. a custom or practice that has existed for a long time _____ _____

Writing Practice

B Circle the correct words or phrases and translate the sentences into your language.

1. Many (literate / **literary**) examples of satire exist throughout the ages.
   ➤ _____

2. The Ig Nobel Prizes are awards (**given** / giving) to recognize unusual scientific achievements.
   ➤ _____

3. Its aim is to hold powerful persons and institutions (into / **up to**) ridicule.
   ➤ _____

4. Their stated purpose is to "honor achievements that make people (**laugh** / laughing)."
   ➤ _____

More Reading Comprehension

C Read the passage and answer the questions.

   A more contemporary example of satire is *Gulliver's Travels* (A) by Irish author Jonathan Swift, which offered a satirical view of English society at that time. In the book, there are two political parties in the story (B) distinguished by the size of their boot heels. This _____ difference between them was Swift's way of satirizing the minor disputes between the two rival political parties of his time. Another famous work of satire is Mark Twain's *The Adventures of Huckleberry Finn*. (C) Written in 1884, just two decades after the American Civil War, the novel mocks the institution of slavery. One of the main characters in the story (D) are Miss Watson, who owns a slave, Jim, even though she considers herself a "good Christian woman" with strong values. Twain uses satire to show the hypocrisy of her owning a slave even though she is a Christian.

1. Which is the most appropriate for the blank?

   a. inconsequential   b. significant   c. major   d. amazing

2. Which one is NOT grammatically correct in the passage?

   a. (A)   b. (B)   c. (C)   d. (D)

Unit 9 19

Unit 10
Natural Factors Influencing Development

Vocabulary Practice

A Write each word or phrase next to its correct definition. Then write its meaning in your language.

merit	afford	tropical	conversely	squalor
exploit	temperate	hinder	appreciable	coincidence
reserve	maritime	renewable	landlocked	at a disadvantage

1. considerable or substantial _____ _____
2. unable to compete equally _____ _____
3. on the other hand; oppositely _____ _____
4. relating to the ocean and ships _____ _____
5. able to be used over and over _____ _____
6. not too hot or too cold; moderate _____ _____
7. very bad or unpleasant conditions _____ _____
8. surrounded by land with no coast _____ _____
9. to treat unfairly or take advantage of _____ _____
10. something that occurs by accident or chance _____ _____
11. a supply of something not needed immediately _____ _____
12. to provide someone with something; to offer _____ _____
13. the characteristic of being good, useful, or beneficial; worth _____ _____
14. describing areas with warm climates near the equator _____ _____
15. to slow down the process of development of something _____ _____

Writing Practice

B Circle the correct words and translate the sentences into your language.

1. Natural factors have an even greater effect (**on** / for) the economies of these nations.

    ➤ _____

2. In addition to geography, a country's location also plays a major role (**in** / on) its development.

    ➤ _____

3. Countries that lack (comparable / **appreciable**) natural resources are at a major economic disadvantage.

    ➤ _____

4. They have developed the infrastructure necessary to (**extract** / extracting) and distribute their vast oil reserves to become wealthy.

    ➤ _____

More Reading Comprehension

C Read the passage and answer the questions.

> Perhaps the most critical factor in a nation's development (A) <u>is</u> its geography. It is not a coincidence that many of the world's poorest nations are located in tropical regions near the equator, (B) <u>where</u> the weather is hot, the land less fertile, and water scarce. Thus, companies do not invest in these countries because they would spend too much money (C) <u>at</u> electricity and other resources to make significant profit. _____, countries located in more temperate regions, such as the United States and many European countries, have had a naturally easier time developing. These places have huge tracts of fertile land, moderate temperatures, and a good amount of rainfall. (D) <u>Due to</u> these factors, companies are more likely to open businesses in such nations since they would have to invest far less time and energy to flourish.

1. Which is the most appropriate for the blank?

    a. Therefore   b. Conversely   c. Otherwise   d. Furthermore

2. Which one is NOT grammatically correct in the passage?

    a. (A)   b. (B)   c. (C)   d. (D)

Unit 11 The Eurasian Eagle-Owl

Vocabulary Practice

A Write each word or phrase next to its correct definition. Then write its meaning in your language.

suit	perch	marsh	striking	formation
dwell	wingspan	mortality	opportunistic	electrocution
keen	encroach	settlement	reintroduce	bird of prey

1. to live in a place _____ _____
2. acute; very developed _____ _____
3. capturing one's attention _____ _____
4. taking advantages of opportunities _____ _____
5. to be appropriate or suitable for _____ _____
6. something that is made or formed _____ _____
7. the death of a person or animal _____ _____
8. a bird that hunts small animals for food _____ _____
9. a place where people have come to live _____ _____
10. the total length of a bird's wings when fully open _____ _____
11. to bring back to a previous state or place; to restore _____ _____
12. an area of wet land that is soft and has a lot of grass _____ _____
13. to move into an area gradually that is outside normal limits _____ _____
14. to sit on something high above ground; a place where a bird sits _____ _____
15. the state of being shocked or killed by a large amount of electricity _____ _____

Writing Practice

B   Circle the correct words or phrases and translate the sentences into your language.

1. Due to its formidable size, the eagle-owl sits (atop / top) the food chain.

    ➤ _____

2. This bird has orange eyes and sharp claws, but it stands (for / out) due to its sheer size.

    ➤ _____

3. Some eagle-owls have (seen / been seen) capturing adult roe deer weighing up to 17 kilograms.

    ➤ _____

4. The eagle-owl can detect even the slightest sounds, enabling it (catch / to catch) its prey effectively.

    ➤ _____

More Reading Comprehension

C   Read the passage and answer the questions.

> ⓐ As human settlements encroach upon eagle-owl territories in Western Europe, the mortality rate of these majestic creatures (A) have increased, (B) with many of them dying from electrocution or flying into electrical towers. ⓑ Perhaps the most prominent example of this occurred from the 1970s to the 1990s in Belgium and Luxembourg, (C) where 1,000 of the birds were reintroduced into nature. ⓒ Studies have shown that this program was successful (D) as the birds were able to breed at rates similar to wild eagle-owls. ⓓ

1. Which is the best place for the sentence?

    > *Therefore, governments and other organizations have been reintroducing the bird since the 1970s.*

    a. ⓐ   b. ⓑ   c. ⓒ   d. ⓓ

2. Which one is NOT grammatically correct in the passage?

    a. (A)   b. (B)   c. (C)   d. (D)

Unit 12: The Works of Louis Pasteur

Vocabulary Practice

A Write each word or phrase next to its correct definition. Then write its meaning in your language.

vat	eradicate	microbe	instrumental	deleterious
lethal	validation	spoilage	plummet	serendipitous
consistently	immunity	sterilize	seize upon	attribute to

1. damaging or harmful _____ _____
2. able to cause death; deadly _____ _____
3. always the same; steadily _____ _____
4. to decrease very rapidly or noticeably _____ _____
5. a large container used for holding liquids _____ _____
6. proof that something is true or correct _____ _____
7. to remove or destroy something completely _____ _____
8. the process or result of rotting or decaying _____ _____
9. to take advantage of something quickly _____ _____
10. very important in causing something to happen _____ _____
11. to say that something is the result of something else _____ _____
12. lucky in finding something beneficial by accident or chance _____ _____
13. the power to keep yourself from being infected by a disease _____ _____
14. to clean something by removing all the germs or bacteria _____ _____
15. a tiny living organism that can only be seen with a microscope _____ _____

Writing Practice

B Circle the correct words or phrases and translate the sentences into your language.

1. To keep this (from / for) happening, he boiled a vat of grape juice to 55 degrees Celsius.
   ➤ _____

2. The process of fermentation converts the sugar from the grapes (into / with) alcohol.
   ➤ _____

3. Louis Pasteur has long (considered / been considered) a giant in the development of modern science.
   ➤ _____

4. His first work was with winemakers who had difficulty (occasionally / consistently) producing quality alcohol.
   ➤ _____

More Reading Comprehension

C Read the passage and answer the questions.

> His greatest discovery was serendipitous. Upon (A) <u>leaving</u> a plate of bacteria out too long, he killed it. ⓐ Deciding (B) <u>to not</u> waste it, he tried injecting healthy chickens with the germs. ⓑ Not only did the chickens not become ill, but they also gained immunity to the disease. ⓒ The use of vaccines was not new as the English physician Edward Jenner (C) <u>had</u> previously discovered a vaccination to prevent smallpox. ⓓ This enabled scientists to protect people from a number of dangerous and potentially life-threatening pathogens. In time, a number of them would be nearly completely (D) <u>eradicated</u>.

1. Which is the best place for the sentence?

   > *Pasteur's work was so monumental because he was able to create vaccines artificially.*

   a. ⓐ   b. ⓑ   c. ⓒ   d. ⓓ

2. Which one is NOT grammatically correct in the passage?

   a. (A)   b. (B)   c. (C)   d. (D)

Unit 12 25

Unit 13

The Difficulty of Predicting Earthquakes

Vocabulary Practice

A Write each word next to its correct definition. Then write its meaning in your language.

shift	install	elusive	impending	geological
crust	seismic	abnormal	diagnostic	magnitude
tremor	odds	prohibitively	precursor	landslide

1. unusual or bizarre _____ _____
2. too much; excessively _____ _____
3. about to happen soon _____ _____
4. a change or alteration _____ _____
5. of or relating to an earthquake _____ _____
6. difficult to find or discover _____ _____
7. related to identifying a problem _____ _____
8. the moving or shaking of the ground _____ _____
9. relating to the study of the Earth _____ _____
10. the outer or topmost layer of the Earth _____ _____
11. the chances or likelihood of something happening _____ _____
12. an event that shows another event is going to happen _____ _____
13. a measurement of the power or intensity of an earthquake _____ _____
14. to put something such as machine somewhere for it to be used _____ _____
15. a large mass of rocks and soil that suddenly moves down a mountain _____ _____

Writing Practice

B Circle the correct words or phrases and translate the sentences into your language.

1. The water in ponds and wells will bubble prior (of / to) earthquakes.

   ➤ _____

2. There are some systems put in place to help people stay safer when an earthquake (do / does) strike.

   ➤ _____

3. This uncertainty in short-term forecasting makes it nearly impossible (generating / to generate) accurate predictions.

   ➤ _____

4. Making more accurate predictions would require scientists to (install / instill) measurement devices several kilometers below ground.

   ➤ _____

More Reading Comprehension

C Read the passage and answer the questions.

> The forecasting of earthquakes remains a prominent area of interest in geological research. (A) <u>By using</u> information collected from global seismic monitoring networks, geological field work, and historical records, seismologists are able to make reasonably accurate forecasts for upcoming years and decades about earthquakes. ___a___, they still lack methods to forecast earthquakes a few days or months (B) <u>in advance</u> accurately. ___b___, earthquake models show that the likelihood of Southern California (C) <u>having</u> an earthquake of a 7.5 magnitude or greater in the next 30 years is 38 percent. However, the same models state that the odds of such a quake happening within a week (D) <u>is</u> only 0.02 percent.

1. Which is the best pair for the blanks?

   a. However ------ Therefore   b. Therefore ------ For instance
   c. However ------ For instance   d. For example ------ However

2. Which one is NOT grammatically correct in the passage?

   a. (A)   b. (B)   c. (C)   d. (D)

Unit 14 Writing Styles Around the World

Vocabulary Practice

A Write each word or phrase next to its correct definition. Then write its meaning in your language.

spiral	thesis	markedly	digression	concession
layout	linguist	premise	formalize	subordination
linear	choppy	peripherally	composition	hone in on

1. to make something official _____ _____
2. a short piece of writing _____ _____
3. noticeably or obviously _____ _____
4. the organization of something _____ _____
5. to focus more on over time _____ _____
6. not flowing smoothly; disconnected _____ _____
7. an admission of a mistake or flaw _____ _____
8. not as the main or important part of something _____ _____
9. going from one thing to another in a direct way _____ _____
10. the sentence in an essay that expresses the main idea _____ _____
11. a person who studies languages and how they are used _____ _____
12. a part of a sentence that acts as a noun, adjective, or adverb _____ _____
13. a basic theory or idea about what something is or how it works _____ _____
14. the act of talking about something that is unrelated to the main point _____ _____
15. a continuous curved line that goes around a central point _____ _____

Writing Practice

B Circle the correct words and translate the sentences into your language.

1. The essay is grouped around a main thesis, (that / **which**) is generally stated near the start.
    ➤ _____

2. It is important (of / **for**) the teacher not to assume that one writing style is superior to another.
    ➤ _____

3. It can be seen (what / **that**) even within related languages, there exists significant diversity.
    ➤ _____

4. English writing focuses on the use of discrete paragraphs with each (**containing** / contained) a single idea.
    ➤ _____

More Reading Comprehension

C Read the passage and answer the questions.

> Not surprisingly, East Asian writing is markedly different from that of English. Most notably, (A) <u>rather than</u> being linear, it is a spiral that eventually (B) <u>hones in on</u> the topic. Asian essays often begin with more general information that is only peripherally related to the main idea. As the composition develops, the writer continually tightens the focus (C) <u>until</u> reaching the main idea. In addition, Asian writers frequently include _____ that raise possible weaknesses in their own arguments. These are not viewed (D) <u>of</u> flaws as they would be in Western-style writing. Instead, they are seen as a reflection of the writer exploring the work in depth.

1. Which is the most appropriate for the blank?

    a. flaws   b. concessions   c. rules   d. digressions

2. Which one is NOT grammatically correct in the passage?

    a. (A)   b. (B)   c. (C)   d. (D)

Unit 15: 3D Printed Organs

Vocabulary Practice

A Write each word or phrase next to its correct definition. Then write its meaning in your language.

fuse	kidney	implant	arrange	in its infancy
rectify	speculate	emulate	develop	transplant
tissue	recreate	run into	cell culture	replacement

1. at the beginning stages
2. to grow together or join
3. to try to be like something
4. to put something in a particular position
5. to make something again; to reproduce
6. to start to have something such as a disease
7. the material that makes up a living creature
8. something added to the body through surgery
9. to experience something such as difficulties
10. something that takes the place of another thing
11. to make a wrong situation become right; to correct
12. a group of cells growing in an artificial environment
13. to think about something and to make guesses about it
14. the organ that removes waste products to clean the blood
15. an operation in which an internal organ of someone is replaced with one from another person

Writing Practice

B Circle the correct words or phrases and translate the sentences into your language.

1. Those who do receive a replacement organ in time might (run out / run into) problems with their bodies rejecting the organ.

    ➤ _____

2. Creating more complex internal organs (has / have) proven too difficult with current technology.

    ➤ _____

3. Scientists have begun (research / researching) methods of applying 3D technology to print organs for transplant.

    ➤ _____

4. One researcher successfully printed and (transplanted / transformed) living bone tissue into artificial jaws.

    ➤ _____

More Reading Comprehension

C Read the passage and answer the questions.

> Most 3D organ printing technology is based on existing 3D printing techniques with some key _____. Instead of using plastic compounds as in other types of 3D printing, researchers use water-based gels (A) <u>containing</u> live cells as ink in 3D printers to layer them in a specific pattern. Over time, the gels break down, and the natural cells expand, (B) <u>growing</u> into full organs. This happens since cells will naturally fuse together (C) <u>when</u> placed in the appropriate pattern and grow into tissue and organs that the body can use. For instance, if you arrange enough ear cells in roughly the correct shape, they will eventually grow into an ear. By allowing nutrients and oxygen (D) <u>for</u> flow through these organs, they can be integrated into the bodies of humans and animals.

1. Which is the most appropriate for the blank?

    a. differences   b. variations   c. similarities   d. movements

2. Which one is NOT grammatically correct in the passage?

    a. (A)   b. (B)   c. (C)   d. (D)

Unit 15 31

Unit 16: Ocean Zones and Their Characteristics

Vocabulary Practice

A Write each word next to its correct definition. Then write its meaning in your language.

term	locate	virtually	volume	camouflage
vent	detritus	coastal	penetrate	remainder
pocket	diversity	ecosystem	hospitable	illumination

1. to find where something is _____ _____
2. nearly, almost, or practically _____ _____
3. to go through or into something _____ _____
4. the rest or what is left over from something _____ _____
5. the amount of space something takes up _____ _____
6. to give something a particular name or meaning _____ _____
7. a small area in which something different is located _____ _____
8. pieces that are left when something breaks, falls apart, etc. _____ _____
9. all the living things that reside in a particular environment _____ _____
10. referring to areas on the edge of a land near the ocean _____ _____
11. the state of having many different types or kinds of something _____ _____
12. an opening through which air, steam, water, etc. can escape _____ _____
13. light that shines into a place, from something, etc. _____ _____
14. to hide something by making it hard to see or by making it look like things around it _____ _____
15. having an environment that makes it easy for plants and animals to live in _____ _____

Writing Practice

B Circle the correct words or phrases and translate the sentences into your language.

1. This ecosystem is still unique and home to a wide (variation / **variety**) of species.

    ➤ _____

2. Because of the wealth of food, over 90 percent of all open ocean life (live / **lives**) in this layer.

    ➤ _____

3. The warm waters and low pressure enable a wide range of life (of surviving / **to survive**).

    ➤ _____

4. As only minimal light reaches this layer, organisms living there have made several remarkable (**adaptations** / adoptions).

    ➤ _____

More Reading Comprehension

C Read the passage and answer the questions.

In the deepest region of the open ocean, the aphotic zone, there are extremely high pressure, near-freezing temperatures, and virtually no light. ⓐ However, improved technology has enabled scientists to dive deep below the open ocean's surface. ⓑ (A)They have found some species that are able to survive by eating the detritus that comes from the upper regions. (B) They have also discovered underground vents, which are cracks in the ocean floor that emit high-temperature water and are rich in chemicals. ⓒ Some bacteria are able to use (C) their hydrogen sulphide in a process that is similar to photosynthesis. Those bacteria can then serve as the basis of an underwater food chain. ⓓ As a result, (D) scientists have located a few pockets of deep-underwater life that display a startling amount of biodiversity.

1. Which is the best place for the sentence?

    > Since these conditions are so harsh, scientists long believed that few species could survive there.

    a. ⓐ b. ⓑ c. ⓒ d. ⓓ

2. Which one refers to something different from the rest?

    a. (A) b. (B) c. (C) d. (D)

Reading Voyage 2

EXPERT

Reading Voyage is an eleven-level reading series divided into four stages: Starter, Basic, Plus, and Expert. The series is designed for high-beginner to low-advanced EFL students who want to enhance their reading abilities. The passages cover a wide range of topics that enable learners to expand their background knowledge. The various exercises will allow students to develop their reading comprehension, critical thinking, and vocabulary skills.

Key Features

- Appealing and informative texts covering a variety of topics
- Vocabulary in Context to help identify word definitions and synonyms
- Comprehension questions to help identify main ideas and details
- Reading Skill and Summary to help students analyze key concepts
- Workbook for additional vocabulary and writing practice

Components

Student Book / Workbook

Download Resources at www.darakwon.co.kr:

MP3 files / Answer Key / Translations / Vocabulary lists

Scan this QR Code for MP3 files

Reading Voyage Series: EXPERT

340-380 words

380-420 words